FINDING JOHN'S JESUS

a meditative journey
for busy people through the words
of John about his Jesus

Scott Evans, Chaplain

Copyright

Finding John's Jesus:

a meditative journey for busy people through the words of John about his Jesus

By Scott Evans, Chaplain

ISBN: 9798535092867
Imprint: Independently published

Available on Amazon

About this Book

John the Writer was the only disciple of Jesus who had the privilege of spending a whole lifetime attempting to unpack who Jesus was after spending three years with him. It is like witnessing a car crash. The accident only takes a few seconds to witness, and then it takes time and processing through the detail of the crash to better understand it.

I'm not saying Jesus was a car wreck. There was just so much to take in after witnessing these powerful accounts of being with God in the neighborhood where the Twelve lived.

John was one of the Twelve Jesus specifically asked, "follow me," walk with me, learn from me while I am here on earth teaching, healing and living out the miracles of God the Father right in front of you. Jesus and the Twelve ate together, traveled together, celebrated life together, worshipped together, prayed together, discussed together, and wept together. John had the privilege of living together with Jesus, the Son of God, who was and is the exact representation of God the Father's very being.

So it took a lifetime for John to unpack and find out who Jesus was.

John writes powerful imagery of who Jesus was. It may have taken him years to put these words to paper because it's difficult to describe something or Someone from another world.

John writes often of Jesus' love. What it takes to love Jesus; how we should love God and those around us; and at the end of the book even asking one of the Twelve if he loved Jesus more than anyone or anything. All of this comes from the writer who referred to himself several times in his writings as "the one Jesus loved."

Maybe all of the Twelve felt that way about Jesus.

It appears that the other three Gospel accounts of Jesus, Matthew, Mark and Luke, were written far earlier than John's account. John took the time to ruminate on Jesus' life even into his 90's before he died exiled on an island. Maybe this is why John wrote about many of the stories the other three authors did not mention. John knew that the Followers of Jesus may have already known those stories well, so he wrote several of the other stories of Jesus' life.

All the Twelve were now dead, and now it was time for John to write his very own account of the life of Jesus which he had the opportunity to process for so many years.

In that process of reliving his life with Jesus he often wrote about love; he wrote about believing and faith, about knowing God and following him and about the whole world. John tells us that Jesus came "for the life of the world."

Today my hope is that through John's accounts and my simple considerations you might "Find John's Jesus."

How to Use this Resource

This resource is an attempt to make the writings and imagery of John more accessible for those of us trying to find Jesus in our busy lives. The passages have been paraphrased in a similar way a pastor might do on a Sunday morning in order to help the Scripture become clear.

John the Writer tells us in great depth who Jesus is. Often his accounts are a bit too much for the time we have to process the full passage. So each entry is broken down into bite-size, digestible chunks to chew on, allowing Jesus to breathe life into us.

Knowing Jesus well can emerge out of mediating on or chewing on Scripture while being in tune with the Spirit of God. Meditation has been described as a chewing on… over and over… in the way a cow chews the grass … and then re-chewing the same grass again to fully digest it.

As you chew on these bite-size accounts of Jesus, may you find the true Jesus John the Writer observed firsthand.

Each entry has the following sections:
An invitation to stop and breathe. A chance to be still before God, to exhale fully and let God fill you.

Then Meditate on the account of Jesus.
Take a moment to read the short paraphrased account from John's writings and meditate on it… chew on it over and over as you breathe in God.

After hearing from God Consider my thoughts.
My simple words are from my own reflections on
this section of John's reflection of Jesus. The goal is
to help the reader better process each account.

**In conclusion, Meditate on the account again, and
go, praying the words God spoke to you.**
Go now, following Jesus and living the life you were
intended to live.

We will begin by skipping the summary about Jesus
at the beginning of John and jumping right into the
stories he records. Then at the end of the book we
will visit John's summary from John 1.

May this Gospel of Jesus help us know God better.
May we all find John's Jesus.

One

Be still before God.
Exhale fully and let God fill you.

Start your time with God today with 'a long exhale.' Let it out; fully exhale in order to breathe in. Breathe in life through your nose. Do it again and again until you are quiet and ready to receive from God. Then let God fill you.

Meditate

John the Baptizer was preaching and baptizing in the wilderness.
They asked who he was.

I am not the Christ, Elijah or the Great Prophet who was predicted to come.

Yet there is One who stands among our people who I am unworthy even to untie his sandals.

Humility

Consider - John 1: 19 - 28

For the moment we will skip John the Writer's opening summary and save it until the end. Let's jump right into the brief backstory of Jesus. His story begins with humility.

Humility is at the very heart of our faith.

This person speaking about Jesus was not John the Writer, but John the Baptizer. Hundreds of years before this story in the Jewish faith (Isaiah 40) God predicted that one would come before the Messiah (the Anointed One of God) to pave the way for him and his message.

John the Baptizer came on the scene and preached repentance. Repentance is the start of embracing Jesus. It is humility, and it is the realization of our need for Jesus to reconcile us to the Father because of our sin.

Humility through repentance is the place John the Writer knew the gospel of Jesus begins. Then and now.

John the Baptizer fully embraced this humility. The people thought he was special, and he was, for he was carrying out his calling. He listened carefully to God and carried out what he was told to do.

He deflected, or redirected, any titles and praise toward Jesus, the One alive and standing among their people by comparing himself to a servant, his servant. A servant who would untie his master's sandals after a long day.

John the Baptizer's role, like ours, is to serve Jesus.

Meditate

John the Baptizer was preaching and baptizing in
the wilderness.
They asked who he was.

I am not the Christ, Elijah or the Great Prophet who
was predicted to come.

Yet there is One who stands among our people who
I am unworthy even to untie his sandals.

Pray and Go

Two

Be still before God.
Exhale fully and let God fill you.

Meditate

John the Baptizer said of Jesus for all to hear,
"Look, that man walking right there towards us, is
the Slaughtered-Lamb from God."

"He takes away the world's sin."

He is the Passover sacrifice
that gives us freedom.

Sacrifice

Consider - John 1: 29 - 34

Sacrifice is also at the very heart of our faith. Our God sacrificed for us.

Although John and Jesus were second cousins, it does not appear that they knew each other. John knew his calling was to prepare a highway for the One coming to rescue us from our sins. John saw what looked like the Spirit of God fluttering down visually from the sky and resting on Jesus. Now John knew who it was he was working for.

John's words of Jesus are odd. He calls Jesus an animal that every Jewish person knew represented freedom. After the Jewish nation spent 400 years of slavery in Egypt, God called Moses to announce rescue and lead them from slavery to freedom. The symbol God chose for freedom at that time was a lamb being sacrificed. The blood was to cover the wooden doorpost of every home. The lamb was eaten that evening, the Angel of Death passed over their home that evening, and the next day they escaped for freedom.

Jesus was the new Slaughtered-Lamb from God to offer freedom to all people living in the slavery of their own sin.

John the Writer later saw Jesus' blood on a wooden cross as the covering for his own sins and the gateway to living free.

Christians follow a God who sacrificed himself for us.

Meditate

John the Baptizer said of Jesus for all to hear,
"Look, that man walking right there toward us is the
Slaughtered-Lamb from God."

"He takes away the world's sin."

He is the Passover sacrifice
that gives us freedom.

Pray and Go

Three

Be still before God.
Exhale fully and let God fill you.

Meditate

Two of John the Baptizer's disciples walked after
Jesus and asked "Where are you living?"

Jesus invited them, "Come,
and see."

After spending the day with Jesus one left and told
his brother, "We have found the Messiah, the
Anointed One promised."

Come and See

Consider - John 1: 35 - 42

Here Jesus invites the curious and creates a culture of "come and see."

Jesus seems to ask people to observe his life, witness his actions, and listen to his words and then let each person decide for themselves who he was.

He did not fully indoctrinate a person with all the facts as soon as he met them, and when a crowd came up he spoke in mysterious stories about the Kingdom of God. There are no formulas to God.

Jesus invited Andrew and his buddy to "come and see."

Jesus also invites us, "come and see."

As you continue reading, may you witness Jesus through the stories he tells and the way he lived. John the Writer witnessed Jesus' life for three years. The Gospel of John is his witness to the world of what he saw and heard… for us to decide.

After the witness of John the Baptizer and being with Jesus for just one day, Andrew knew that Jesus was the One Promised from long ago to rescue his Jewish Nation from oppression and the world from its present darkness.

Meditate

Two of John the Baptizer's disciples walked after Jesus and asked "Where are you living?"

Jesus invited them, "Come,
and see."

After spending the day with Jesus one left and told his brother, "We have found the Messiah, the Anointed One promised."

Pray and Go

Four

Be still before God.
Exhale fully and let God fill you.

Meditate

Jesus was ready to leave Galilee, so he found Philip and said to him, "follow me."

Philip immediately found Nathaniel and said to him, "Come and see. We have found the One Moses and the prophets said was coming."

Nathaniel came and saw Jesus... and believed it to be true.

Follow Me

Consider - John 1: 43 - 51

Jesus continues his simple words to common people by just asking them to come along, check him out, and then choose to figure out what to do with the reality of him.

In our religious world we seem to make everything complicated, ... or maybe just religious. We miss the simple realities of Jesus inviting people in and asking them to walk with him and consider who he is. If Jesus is life, why not choose life in and through Jesus.

Consider who Scripture says Jesus is in your meditations today.

In yesterday's and today's meditations, Andrew, then Simon, Philip, and Nathaniel came, saw, and followed Jesus. These men knew the promises of the Old Testament. They all experienced a three-year journey of a lifetime that launched their own taking of the message of Jesus to their world. They were all martyred for their message.

"Come and see." - Jesus.

"Follow me." - Jesus.

They could not keep it in after meeting Jesus and had to tell another.

Follow Jesus. Tell another.

Meditate

Jesus was ready to leave Galilee, so he found Philip and said to him, "follow me."

Philip immediately found Nathaniel and said to him, "Come and see. We have found the One Moses and the prophets said was coming."

Nathaniel came and saw Jesus… and believed it to be true.

Pray and Go

Five

Be still before God.
Exhale fully and let God fill you.

Meditate

In a nearby place, Jesus and company were at a huge
wedding celebration.

His mother Mary noticed a problem; the celebration
was out of wine.
She looks to Jesus to solve the problem.

Was Jesus not quite ready, was it now his time…
Mary hints for him to perform a miracle.

Jesus listens, hesitates… then he honors her.

He involves the servants in the miracle by asking
them to fill the six thirty-gallon pots with water.
All of a sudden it becomes good wine.
Not only just wine, but the best of all wine.

Honoring Others

Consider - John 2: 1 - 11

The time was rapidly approaching for Jesus to reveal himself to the world. Mary may have felt it, or maybe she just saw in Jesus his desire to help others.

Mary involves Jesus. Jesus appears hesitant.

The next three years of Jesus' life and work would would begin a revolution.

It would be super difficult. He would be always questioned; he would be a traveling preacher with dusty feet; he would have many long days and tiring journeys; he would rely on food from God provided by others; he would touch people with skin diseases and everyone wanted a piece of him... heading all the way to his crucifixion.

Jesus knew the struggle coming. Was it time to reveal his glory?

The very heart of this story of Jesus is the way a son honored his mother, in front of his peers, in a male dominant world, ... obeying his Jewish roots and one of the Ten Commandments of honoring his father and mother.

Jesus began a revolution by honoring others.

He submitted to his mother and honored her and her request. He honored the people at the wedding. John had the privilege of observing how Jesus honored people. He was the only writer to record this Gospel story. The revolution has now begun.

Meditate

In a nearby place, Jesus and company were at a huge
wedding celebration.

His mother Mary noticed a problem, the celebration
was out of wine.
She looks to Jesus to solve the problem.

Was Jesus not quite ready, was it now his time…
Mary hints for him to perform a miracle.

Jesus listens, hesitates… then he honors her.

He involves the servants in the miracle by asking
them to fill the six, thirty-gallon pots with water.
All of a sudden it becomes good wine.
Not only just wine, but the best of all wine.

Pray and Go

Six

Be still before God.
Exhale fully and let God fill you.

Meditate

Jesus was now in Jerusalem for the coming
Passover-freedom celebration.

In the temple courts of his Father's House, men
were selling cattle and doves for sacrifice and acting
like an ATM for other worshippers.

Jesus made a whip.
He drove out all the cattle, and the birds flew away.
With zeal he flipped the ATM tables and
drove out the merchants saying,
"How dare you make the place we meet with my
Father into a market!"

My Father's House

Consider - John 2: 12 - 25

The temple courts were meant to be the place the People of God would go to meet with God. Jesus saw this as a special, very personal place.

Jesus was often found in the courts of his Father praying, listening, and teaching. It was a beautiful place to be close to his Father.

The courts, it appears, were turned into a market for selling animals for sacrifice to satisfy the Old Jewish Law. People were even turning a profit.

Jesus was angry. Anger is a natural-given desire God has installed in us all to fight injustice in the world. If you see an adult beating a child, God instilled in you the emotion of anger for you to do something about it.

After he drove out the merchants, he was asked who gave him the authority to do this. He was disrupting the system... the way things worked. The Jewish leaders asked for a sign, something supernatural, to prove he had the authority from God.

Jesus speaks in hyperbole. "You will destroy this temple (pointing to his own body) and it will only take me three days to rebuild it." Today we know that this reference was about his coming crucifixion and resurrection.

The connection was that Jesus' body, or house, became the place through which we too can meet with God.

Be with our Father today in Jesus.

Meditate

Jesus was in Jerusalem for the coming Passover-
freedom celebration.

In the temple courts of his Father's House, men
were selling cattle and doves for sacrifice and acting
like an ATM for other worshippers.

Jesus made a whip.
He drove out all the cattle and the birds flew away.
With zeal he flipped the ATM tables and
drove out the merchants saying,
"How dare you make the place we meet with my
Father into a market!"

Pray and Go

Seven

Be still before God.
Exhale fully and let God fill you.

Meditate

Nick knocked on Jesus' door after dark with a
question;
"Based on what you have done, it looks like you are
from God!?"

Jesus responds, "You cannot see his kingdom
without being reborn."

Nick asks, "But how, birth happens once?"

Jesus responds, "There is another birth; the second
birth is a Spiritual birth.
You must be reborn to see God at work.
One born of the Spirit is like the wind."

Reborn

Consider - John 3: 1 - 8

Here Jesus is answering Nick's (short for Nicodemus) question with metaphors. Nick was digging in and trying to find answers to his questions. He was taking a big risk as a religious leader coming to Jesus.

His question basically was, "Who are you?"

Jesus seldom answers questions directly. The metaphors he uses are in being reborn and also the evidence of wind. We can't see wind, but we can see what it moves. The wind here seems to be the result of the Spirit of God leading and working in one who has been reborn.

We need to be reborn because we are told we are dead. All of us are dead in our sin. We need to be reborn by God.

Jesus does not yet tell Nick, or us, how to be reborn. Stop. Pause. Listen to God.

In the next entry Jesus will enlighten us on the way to be reborn and made new.

Then stay tuned throughout the book of John to see if Nick becomes reborn. He is mentioned later in John 7 and John 19.

May Jesus give us life.

Meditate

Nick knocked on Jesus' door after dark with a
question;
"Based on what you have done, it looks like you are
from God!?"

Jesus responds, "You cannot see his kingdom
without being reborn."

Nick asks, "But how, birth happens once?"

Jesus responds, "There is another birth; the second
birth is a Spiritual birth.
You must be reborn to see God at work.
One born of the Spirit is like the wind."

Pray and Go

Eight

Be still before God.
Exhale fully and let God fill you.

Meditate

Nick, do you remember the story of our ancestors
when they complained about their lack of food
while having new freedom in the desert? God sent
them poisonous snakes.

But then he also provided rescue. God had Moses
fasten a bronze snake on a pole saying,
"If bitten, look and live!"

If they looked at the bronze serpent, it showed they
believed God would rescue them from death.

The same is true with me. I, the Son of Man, must
be lifted up on a pole.
Anyone who looks at me and believes will have life,
real life, everlasting life.

Look and Believe

Consider - John 3: 10 - 15

In order to teach Nick what was necessary for rebirth, he used an Old Testament story they both knew. It is found in Numbers 21.

The story was about their people's sin and the penalty for it; judgment by God and death.

When the people cried out to God for rescue, God provided it in the form of a bronze snake.

In the Garden of Eden, the first of our race went from immortality to becoming mortal because of his sin. This is where we all find ourselves before Jesus.

We, like Adam, have eaten the apple and will die. Our sin is awfully destructive. It wrecks us, our neighborhoods, the world, and separates us from the life-sustaining love of God.

Sin is our choice.

Jesus is God's intervention, his Rescuer for us to live.

Look in faith to Jesus and live.

Meditate

Nick, do you remember the story of our ancestors when they complained about their lack of food while having new freedom in the desert? God sent them poisonous snakes.

But then he also provided rescue. God had Moses fasten a bronze snake on a pole saying,
"If bitten, look and live!"

If they looked at the bronze serpent, it showed they believed God would rescue them from death.

The same is true with me. I, the Son of Man, must be lifted up on a pole.
Anyone who looks at me and believes will have life, real life, everlasting life.

Pray and Go

Nine

Be still before God.
Exhale fully and let God fill you.

Meditate

"Nick, here is the story we all live in.
God so much loved all of this, the Cosmos,
that he gave his only Son.

Whoever looks to him for rescue and believes,
like the bronze serpent,
will never truly die and will have now and never-
ending life.

I, God's Son, did not come here to condemn the
world,
but to rescue this already-condemned-by-your-own-
choices world." - Jesus

God so loved… he gave

Consider - John 3: 16 - 21

Jesus' words to Nick use the story of the bronze snake to show him how to find rebirth and answer his initial question, "Are you from God?"

At the very foundation of this story is God and how much he loves everything in this well-ordered universe. God loves what he made. He loves what he is sustaining.

He rescues what is his.

The problem is our sin. My sin is destructive and is hurting your life and wrecking the cosmos. We can see it in my excessive consumption leaving a large carbon footprint, my plastic washing up on someone else's shores, or in my judgment of my neighbors and withholding love. But is my judgment of another visible in the stars or trees?

In Romans chapter 8 we are told that all of creation, the trees, etc., is waiting for the day it is liberated and freed from the bondage of decay placed on it by our sin. Our sin broke our relationship with our God and harmed the trees.

God so much loved all of this and us in our sin... that he gave us his Son to be sacrificed on a pole so all who look to him and believe will really live now and forever with him. Jesus' return will mark a true liberation for us and the trees.

God so loved the Cosmos, he gave us Jesus.

Meditate

"Nick, here is the story we all live in.
God so much loved all of this, the Cosmos,
that he gave his only Son.

Whoever looks to him for rescue and believes,
like the bronze serpent,
will never truly die and have now and never-ending
life.

I, God's Son, did not come here to condemn the
world,
but to rescue this already-condemned-by-your-own-
choices world." - Jesus

Pray and Go

Ten

Be still before God.
Exhale fully and let God fill you.

Meditate

John the Baptizer was told by some that Jesus was taking over his business and baptizing more people.

John the Baptizer's response; "I know my calling and my place. I am like the Best Man taking care of the Groom on his wedding day. My work is to make him look great on that day.

The Groom has now received all authority from the Father. The Father loves him.
Look to the Son and not me;
believe in him to find real life."

Calling

Consider - John 3: 22 - 36

Finding our calling in life often seems like an overwhelming task. It can seem like a mystery, but our God is a Father who wishes to give good things to his children. He is not trying to hide your calling from you.

What can we see from John's perspective?

John had a very specific calling; to prepare the way for Jesus; and yet it connects to all of us. His work was to show others Jesus. Isn't that the calling for every one of his followers?!

John pointed people to Jesus.

John humbly knew his place. He was okay with being second to Jesus. John knew that it was God who elevates people.

John did not "own" this work. John baptized, then he was okay with Jesus and others doing the same work. He called all people to repent from their selfish lives and be dunked in water as a sign of their repentance. He did not care who did it. He just stayed faithful to what his calling was. He was a team player.

It was now the wedding day. Look to the Groom to find real life... and your calling.

Meditate

John the Baptizer was told by some that Jesus now was taking over his business and baptizing more people.

John the Baptizer's response, "I know my calling and my place. I am like the Best Man taking care of the Groom on his wedding day. My work is to make him look great on that day.

The Groom has now received all authority from the Father. The Father loves him.
Look to the Son and not me;
believe in him to find real life."

Pray and Go

Eleven

Be still before God.
Exhale fully and let God fill you.

Meditate

Jesus, exhausted from the journey on foot, rested at a hand-dug well.
It was mid-afternoon, and a woman came out from town to get water.

Thirsty, Jesus asked her kindly for a drink, for he had no bucket to lower.

Shocked, the woman looked at Jesus because she knew that Jewish people considered her people half-breeds and looked down on them.

They would not talk to her people, but Jesus did.

Broke down walls

Consider - John 4: 1 - 9

John the Writer carefully observed Jesus for three years, and this was a story that showed him so much about the heart of his Teacher. This story is not told elsewhere in the other three Gospels.

In this story we see Jesus tired and thirsty from a long journey on foot. One observation John records about Jesus was that he had human, physical needs. He had the same skin we have; he breathed the same air we breathe and grew physically tired and thirsty. It is as if God walked here in our shoes.

Jesus was like any one of us. Jesus was like every one of us.

Jesus came into our villages to rescue us and to show us how we were made to live.

Jesus broke down the walls dividing people.

The conflicts we have with people because of race is ridiculous in the eyes of Jesus. Jesus made everything and everyone. God so loved the whole world; Jesus came for all who would believe; he died for the life of the world.

We are all the same standing before our God.

In this account, Jesus was tired, exhausted and still chose to break down the walls that divide us… to offer this woman life… stay tuned for the rest of the story.

Meditate

Jesus, exhausted from the journey on foot, rested at a hand-dug well.
It was mid-afternoon and a woman came out from town to get water.

Thirsty, Jesus asked her kindly for a drink, for he had no bucket to lower.

Shocked, the woman looked at Jesus because she knew that Jewish people considered her people half-breeds and looked down on them.

They would not talk to her people, but Jesus did.

Pray and Go

Twelve

Be still before God.
Exhale fully and let God fill you.

Meditate

Jesus and this half-Jewish woman continue their talk
at the well.

Jesus said, "If you had any idea who I am or a clue
about the good gifts God gives,
you would have asked me for water."

The woman replied, "You don't have a bucket!"

Jesus said, "The water I offer satisfies for life. It will
continue to bubble up within you, reviving you to
really live."

The woman pleaded, "Sir, I want this Living Water."

Living Water

Consider - John 4: 1 - 15

700 years before Jesus walked on the earth in Isaiah 55, God offers us Living Water to those who are thirsty. This water was obviously different than the water we drink daily.

The body needs water over and over again to live. God's water is satisfying, nourishing, and gives never-ending life. God invites us to drink.

Jesus continues to dialogue with this woman when other Jewish people would not associate with her. Although he was actually thirsty, he continued to have this conversation and use this language from Isaiah 55 to open her heart and care for her and her soul.

John the Writer saw that Jesus ...

had compassion for those needing rescue,

cared about women,

loved those not in the church.

Jesus offered her real and never-ending water to drink. This water was himself. This water was life.

Jesus did not ask her to stop drinking water. He asked her to reconsider the water she desired.

Want Jesus? Drink of the Living Water.

Meditate

Jesus and this half-Jewish woman continue their talk
at the well.

Jesus said, "If you had any idea who I am or a clue
about the good gifts God gives,
you would have asked me for water."

The woman replied, "You don't have a bucket!"

Jesus said, "The water I offer satisfies for life. It will
continue to bubble up within you reviving you to
really live."

The woman pleaded, "Sir, I want this Living Water."

Pray and Go

Thirteen

Be still before God.
Exhale fully and let God fill you.

Meditate

Our conversation at the well continues as
Jesus asks the woman to go and get her husband.

Her life was exposed by his request. She had many
husbands and was never satisfied with one. She
needed Living Water.

Realizing that Jesus already knew this, she now said,
"You are a prophet! Where should we worship…
this mountain or in Jerusalem?"

Jesus responds, "The time is now for pure worship of
God to happen anytime / everywhere.
God is spirit.
Pure worship happens in your spirit and by living
God's truth.
He seeks this type of worshipper."

Exposed

Consider - John 4: 16 - 26

Exposed.

Jesus has a way of exposing our hearts. Here, by a simple statement, Jesus exposes the heart of this Samaritan woman. "Go and get your husband."

Her life was exposed. One man was never good enough. She was never satisfied. But she was searching. She knew where her people worshipped God… and possibly worshipped with them. She also knew where Jewish people worshipped. She knew the Jewish promise of a coming Messiah, the One predicted to come and rescue the world.

Her life was exposed, and Jesus stayed right there with her.

Here we also find worship being exposed.

In her mind, worship was a place. Places on this mountain or in the temple Jerusalem. Jesus exposes and re-defines worship as far more than religion.

Jesus tells us that people who practicing pure worship do it in their spirit and by living God's truth.

Pure and true worship happens "24 / 7." It doesn't only happen on Saturdays or Sundays.

To see Jesus clearly exposes our hearts to worship him. Only when our lives our exposed can we live pure worship to our God.

Meditate

Our conversation at the well continues as
Jesus asks the woman to go and get her husband.

Her life was exposed by his request. She had many
husbands and was never satisfied with one. She
needed Living Water.

Realizing that Jesus already knew this, she now said,
"You are a prophet! Where should we worship…
this mountain or in Jerusalem?"

Jesus responds, "The time is now for pure worship of
God to happen anytime / everywhere.
God is spirit.
Pure worship happens in your spirit and by living
God's truth.
He seeks this type of worshipper."

Pray and Go

Fourteen

Be still before God.
Exhale fully and let God fill you.

Meditate

The woman at the well tells Jesus, "I know the
Messiah is coming. Then it will all make sense."
Jesus replies, "I am the Messiah."

The disciples return with food and wonder why
Jesus is talking to this woman. They know he is tired
and hungry and offer him food. The woman is
shocked by Jesus' statement and runs off to tell
everyone in her town.

Jesus responds to the Twelve; "I have food that you
are clueless about. My food is doing what God
requests. This is my work, this is my food."

Because of the woman's words, many Samaritans
from town come out to Jesus and believe, saying,
"this man is the Savior of the world."

Tell

Consider - John 4: 25 - 42

Jesus reveals who he is to this half-Jewish-sinning woman. The amazing thing about Jesus is that he came to save those of us who know we are sinners. Jesus seemed to have problems with those who did not feel they were sinners.

My guess is that if you asked this woman if she was a sinner, her answer would have been, "Yes!" She knew it; she knew she was missing something more. She was living with various men to find intimacy and love, and spiritually she desired more too. She seemed to be seeking answers… from their religion and longing for this Promised Messiah from God who would come and rescue. Quite possibly she was running away from her religion that provided her with rules but did not provide her with meaning. She knew she her life was opposed to that religion… and she longed for more. She knew she needed rescue.

She met Jesus (her Messiah and Savior), believed and told everyone she knew.

Who was this Jesus that John is writing about in this story?
* Jesus was human, tired and hungry.
* Jesus was the Promised Messiah.
* Jesus was the Rescuer / Savior of the World.
* Jesus was full of compassion for sinners.

Know we are sinners. Receive the Living Water Jesus offers. Then tell other sinners where to find rescue.

Meditate

The woman at the well tells Jesus, "I know the Messiah is coming. Then it will all make sense."

Jesus replies, "I am the Messiah."

The disciples return with food and wonder why Jesus is talking to this woman. They know he is tired and hungry and offer him food. The woman is shocked by Jesus' statement and runs off to tell everyone in her town.

Jesus responds to the Twelve, "I have food that you are clueless about. My food is doing what God requests. This is my work, this is my food."

Because of the woman's words, many Samaritans from town come out to Jesus and believe, saying, "this man is the Savior of the world."

Pray and Go

Fifteen

Be still before God.
Exhale fully and let God fill you.

Meditate

Jesus has now returned to the place he grew up after living two days with the Samaritans.

In Samaria they listened to his words, but here they only came because of his miracles. Jesus was frustrated.

While there, a governor from a local town sought out Jesus. He said, "My son is nearly dead; I beg you to come and heal him. Please come before he dies."

Jesus said, "Your son is now healed. Go home and see."

The father believed what Jesus said and went home. He found his son healed at the exact time Jesus spoke to him. Now he and his whole household believed in Jesus.

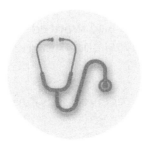

Heart-Belief

Consider - John 4: 43 - 54

So many of us have felt at one point that if we could just see Jesus, and see him do miracles, we would believe,… or believe more. In this passage we are beginning to see that seeing does not always equal believing.

How do we believe, with our eyes, minds or with our hearts? Some doctors still use a stethoscope to hear the beat of a person's heart. Why? They know it must still be beating because their patient is alive, but they want to know how it is beating.

Belief also comes from deep inside us.

In the foreign land of Samaria, Jesus hung out with people who were looked down on and considered pure-Jewish. They were looking for the coming Messiah with open hearts. They desired God's rescue. Once they met and heard Jesus they believed in him.

Back in Jesus' hometown, his neighbors appeared to have been unable to believe because they saw Jesus as a carpenter. They were full of their own religion and absent of truly seeking God. They failed to receive Jesus' words and wanted signs. They wanted to see with their eyes, and their hearts were far from God.

How do you and I receive Jesus? Are we desperately seeking him?

Later in this story, a father was desperate. He had nowhere else to go, so he ran to Jesus. He was desperate and he believed.

Meditate

Jesus has now returned to the place he grew up after living two days with the Samaritans.

In Samaria they listened to his words, but here they only came because of his miracles. Jesus was frustrated.

While there, a governor from a local town sought out Jesus. He said, "My son is nearly dead, I beg you to come and heal him. Please come before he dies."

Jesus said, "Your son is now healed. Go home and see."

The father believed what Jesus said and went home. He found his son healed at the exact time Jesus spoke to him. Now he and his whole household believed in Jesus.

Pray and Go

Sixteen

Be still before God.
Exhale fully and let God fill you.

Meditate

A Jewish religious feast in Jerusalem was to begin.
As was Jesus' practice, he headed into the city for
the feast. While there he chose to go to a pool
where disabled people would gather. Jesus walked
among the needy.

There he saw a man who had not walked for 38
years. He learned this by inquiring about his story.
Then he spoke to him, "Do you want to be healed?"

The man said he has no one to help him into the
pool. They all believed the waters had healing
powers when it began to move.

Jesus said, "Stand and walk. Don't forget to take
your mat."
Immediately the man jumped up like any healthy
person and walked.

Compassion

Consider - John 5: 1 - 10

Compassion inquires. Wouldn't it be cool to have the power to heal?

Jesus obviously did, and yet in this story he inquired about the story of this specific man. Then he did not assume he wished to be healed but asked him.

God cares about our stories and does not force his goodness on us. John the Writer saw compassion in the Son of God.

There is mystery in the story about this famed pool. Did the stirring of the water actually bring healing or was it just legend? Why didn't Jesus heal everyone there? His message was the reason he came, yet he could not help himself to heal, or re-create, a person in need.

For those of us who are reading this passage today and know God, why are we so privileged? God's work is mysterious. Those of us who he has compassion on must be grateful.

Jesus heals the man and then slips through the crowd and leaves.

Meditate

A Jewish religious feast in Jerusalem was to begin. As was Jesus' practice he headed into the city for the feast. While there he chose to go to a pool where disabled people would gather. Jesus walked among the needy.

There he saw a man who had not walked for 38 years. He learned this by inquiring about his story. Then he spoke to him, "Do you want to be healed?"

The man said he has no one to help him into the pool. They all believed the waters had healing powers when it began to move.

Jesus said, "Stand and walk. Don't forget to take your mat."
Immediately the man jumped up like any healthy person and walked.

Pray and Go

Seventeen

Be still before God.
Exhale fully and let God fill you.

Meditate

The religious leaders found this formerly paralyzed man walking on the Sabbath-Rest Day carrying a mat. They said, "That's against our laws! Why?"

The man said, "Some guy healed me and told me to do it."

"Who?" they asked.

The healed man replied he had no idea.

Later Jesus re-found the man in the temple and told him to stop sinning. The look of "Huh?" was on the man's face.

It was obvious; God healed him. Give him honor. He went and told the religious leaders it was Jesus.

Missing miracles

Consider - John 5: 11 - 15

John the Writer saw Jesus as One who carried out the Father's work. He also saw Jesus as One who always gave the Father the honor for all he did.

The religious leaders' rules were so rigid that 'even miracles' were not allowed on their Religious-Rest-Day. Later in this passage we are told God is 'always working,' even on the Sabbath-Rest Day.

The unspoken words of Jesus here were for the man to quit missing that God brought about this miracle. This man did not know who the person was that healed him, but if he had taken a step back, he should have realized it was ultimately from God.

When we are blessed, the blessing is ultimately from God. Give him the honor.

We often miss both the small and the large miracles in our own lives. We pray for someone and forget to thank God after they are well. Many of us have food to eat and clean water to drink today. Don't miss the small miracles.

We have the gift of life and many of us have the ability to walk. Though someone reading this today may not be able to walk. We pray for your healing; we pray for God's grace in your life.

As we go through the day today may we discover both God's large and small miracles.

Meditate

The religious leaders found this formerly paralyzed man walking on the Sabbath-Rest-Day carrying a mat. They said, "That's against our laws! Why?"

The man said, "Some guy healed me and told me to do it."

"Who?" they asked.

The healed man replied he had no idea.

Later Jesus re-found the man in the temple and told him to stop sinning. The look of "Huh?" was on the man's face.

It was obvious, God healed him. Give him honor. He went and told the religious leaders it was Jesus.

Pray and Go

Eighteen

Be still before God.
Exhale fully and let God fill you.

Meditate

Because of this healing the religious Jews hated Jesus, and after the following statement began to try and kill him. "I am always working like my Father who still is working since Creation to this very day."

In their minds the two sins of Jesus were his doing good on the Sabbath-Rest Day and saying he was equal to God the Father. Both of these were the truth.

Jesus said, "Look at a family in these parts. When you observe a son, you will find him doing the family business just like his dad. I am also doing exactly what my Father is doing. He loves me and reveals to me what he is up to.

He is handing over to me the family business."

Always Working

Consider - John 5: 16 - 23

Jesus has been handed the family business and his Father's continuing work.

Just consider when we look at nature and consider the way this world keeps on rolling; gravity stays in place, love breathes life into us, birds know when to migrate, and we get to breathe, … and then breathe again, that God made all this and keeps it running.

It is fascinating to consider that God is 'still working' in all of this, sustaining it, giving it life and holding it all together.

While Jesus walked on this earth he continued to do his Father's work in revealing to us a little of what his desired restoration of all things looks like. Our good-God desires good again in us both physically and spiritually.

When faced with the choice of following the rules of their Jewish religion or giving life to a paralyzed man … he chose life.

It is so encouraging to follow and serve a God who gives us good gifts and also wants us to give others good gifts.

The Father is always working and doing good, the Son is always doing good, and those of us in 'the family business' are invited to always be doing good too.

Meditate

Because of this healing the religious Jews hated Jesus, and after the following statement began to try and kill him. "I am always working like my Father who still is working since Creation to this very day."

In their minds the two sins of Jesus were his doing good on the Sabbath-Rest Day and saying he was equal to God the Father. Both of these were the truth.

Jesus said, "Look at a family in these parts. When you observe a son, you will find him doing the family business just like his dad. I am also doing exactly what my Father is doing. He loves me and reveals to me what he is up to.

He is handing over to me the family business."

Pray and Go

Nineteen

Be still before God.
Exhale fully and let God fill you.

Meditate

Jesus said, "The Father is handing over to me the family business… he gives life and so do I.
He even handed 'the day of judgment' over to me, although I have now come to save.

Hear my words, believe God and have now and never-ending life.
This is how you cross over the bridge from death to life.

Someday the dead will rise when they hear my voice. They will come out of the grave and live.

Those who have 'done good' will live.
Those who have 'done evil' will be judged."

Death to Life

Consider - John 5: 24 - 30

Crossing over from death to life is something offered to us by Jesus. This is more than an idea; it is an actual rebirth and crossing over to immortal living.

One can think of this immortality we are offered like the death and resurrection of Jesus. He physically died and then was physically raised in a new body to life never-ending.

We too are offered this same never-ending life in Jesus. This is what it means to cross over from death to life. Death no longer has dominance over us. Death is no longer our final end. Life in Jesus makes us a new creation.

The Father passed the ability on to Jesus to freely offer life to us. Jesus gives life.

Based on Jesus' words, this life, or eternally living, comes to people who do two things;
we must hear his words as from God and believe in him enough for 'good' actions to come out of our lives.

Doing good was what Jesus had just been accused of doing on this Sabbath day.

Cross over from the judgment of death to life never-ending.

Meditate

Jesus said, "The Father is handing over to me the family business… he gives life and so do I.
He even handed 'the day of judgment' over to me, although I have now come to save.

Hear my words; believe God and have now and never-ending life.
This is how you cross over the bridge from death to life.

Someday the dead will rise when they hear my voice. They will come out of the grave and live.

Those who have 'done good' will live.
Those who have 'done evil' will be judged."

Pray and Go

Twenty

Be still before God.
Exhale fully and let God fill you.

Meditate

Jesus spoke to the religious, non-believing Jewish
leaders,
"You seek out the praise of men, but do not have the
love of God in your hearts.
You say you follow Moses, you diligently study his
writings and the Holy Scriptures, and
you think that your learning gives you never-ending
life.

Moses writings and the Scriptures point to me
and scream my Name,
and you missed it. You don't believe.

John the Baptizer pointed to me.
He was a brilliant light that burned to give you light
and you missed it."

Brilliant Light

Consider - John 5: 31 - 47

John the Writer continues to record Jesus' conversations with the group of antagonists that followed Jesus around to argue. They were religious and considered themselves experts in the Old Testament writings and the laws given by Moses.

Yet even with their large amounts of learning they did not have the love of God in their hearts. Knowing God comes from far more than factual knowledge. They missed the heart of God and the intent of the Law. They missed the larger story of what God was doing in the world … and they missed who Jesus was.

In contrast, John the Baptizer was a brilliant burning light that pointed to Jesus. He was humble and not concerned with the praise from other men. He merely and clearly carried out why God put him here on earth.

Seeking out the praise of others can and will trip us up.

This book and, even more, the writings of Scriptures exist to point us to Jesus.

Only Jesus!

Meditate

Jesus spoke to the religious, non-believing Jewish leaders,
"You seek out the praise of men, but do not have the love of God in your hearts.
You say you follow Moses, you diligently study his writings and the Holy Scriptures, and
you think that your learning gives you never-ending life.

Moses writings and the Scriptures point to me,
and scream my Name,
and you missed it. You don't believe.

John the Baptizer pointed to me.
He was a brilliant light that burned to give you light and you missed it."

Pray and Go

Twenty-one

Be still before God.
Exhale fully and let God fill you.

Meditate

Jesus sought solitude with the Twelve on a
mountain, but a 5,000+ crowd who had witnessed
his miracles followed him to that spot.

Jesus turned to Philip and asked, "Where can we buy
'enough' food for everyone?" … while having a plan.

Andrew discovered a boy near the front of the
crowd who had a lunch of five loaves of bread and
two fish. Then Andrew added that wouldn't be
'enough.'

Jesus had them sit in the grass,
gave thanks to the Father,
and they handed out 'enough' food for all the people
plus twelve basketfuls left over.

There was 'enough.'

Enough

Consider - John 6: 1 - 15

Consider the size of the crowd. Someone estimated 5,000 men plus women and children. This could have been 10,000 people. Imagine that many people finding you and walking up to you, not in a stadium, but in a remote area. They had witnessed or heard of Jesus' great miracles, but would Jesus be enough for them today. They may not have even considered their need for food; possibly they just needed to be with Jesus.

Consider the times. There were no supermarkets to buy food for large groups. Refrigeration did not exist and Amazon did not deliver the same day.

Consider the remote location. Jesus was alongside a large lake in a remote area. Villages were in walking distance, but the only thing here really was Jesus.

They only sought Jesus and he was 'enough.'

Here again John the Writer witnessed Jesus turning to the Father in gratitude and then seeing miracles happen.

The crowd may not have even expected food; why would they? Then they witnessed the food continually coming from the place Jesus was.

When they left that day, all they knew was that they sought Jesus and had 'enough.'

Seek Jesus, be grateful and that will be 'enough' for today.

Meditate

Jesus sought solitude with the Twelve on a mountain, but a 5,000+ crowd who had witnessed his miracles followed him to that spot.

Jesus turned to Philip and asked, "Where can we buy 'enough' food for everyone?" … while having a plan.

Andrew discovered a boy near the front of the crowd who had a lunch of five loaves of bread and two fish. Then Andrew added that wouldn't be 'enough.'

Jesus had them sit in the grass,
gave thanks to the Father,
and they handed out 'enough' food for all the people plus twelve basketfuls left over.

There was 'enough.'

Pray and Go

Be still before God.
Exhale fully and let God fill you.

Meditate

After feeding the 5,000+ crowd it was now evening, and Jesus slipped away from the crowd and went up into the mountain. He sent his twelve to their next location in a boat across the great lake.

The Twelve were three miles out and the rowing got tough. Darkness was all around them. Strong winds blew; the waves grew choppy rocking the boat. Jesus was not with them. Or was he?

Then they saw him. It looked as if he was walking on the waves.
They were terrified!
In their terror Jesus spoke, "It's me; have no fear."

They helped him into the boat and all of a sudden they arrived at their port to find rest.

Waves

Consider - John 6: 16 - 24

Consider the darkness of the middle of the night in a small boat on the sea. Now add waves rocking your boat. Although some of these guys were fishermen, the combination of darkness, a storm, tiredness in rowing and no Jesus allowed them to fixate on the waves continually hitting the boat.

Why is it that when we are tired, distracted, or being rocked by the storms in our lives we forget Jesus is here? We forget he is present with us.

The whole story of Scripture is about our God being with us ... he is continually present, he is always working toward bringing redemption and restoration to his people.

He wants us to be with him.
* Even in the judgment of the Flood, consider the hope in the provision of Noah's large barge preserving the future of our race.
 * See Abraham being promised that through him the world would be blessed and then seeing God stick with his people in Scripture even when they turned on him.
* Witness the rescue in Exodus of one million of God's people out of slavery.
* All of this points toward Jesus' coming here to be present with us so we can be present with God.

John the Writer felt the waves hitting the boat and experienced Jesus' strong presence in his time of need. Jesus is still here.

Meditate

After feeding the 5,000+ crowd it was now evening and Jesus slipped away from the crowd and went up into the mountain. He sent his twelve to their next location in a boat across the great lake.

The Twelve were three miles out and the rowing got tough. Darkness was all around them. Strong winds blew; the waves grew choppy rocking the boat. Jesus was not with them. Or was he?

Then they saw him. It looked as if he was walking on the waves.
They were terrified!
In their terror Jesus spoke, "It's me, have no fear."

They helped him into the boat and all of a sudden they arrived at their port to find rest.

Pray and Go

Be still before God.
Exhale fully and let God fill you.

Meditate

The crowd that chased Jesus around the lake acted like they were out for a stroll and just bumped into him asking, "Teacher, when did you arrive?"

Jesus saw through them and told them they were following him for free food and not to see the works of God he was doing.

Jesus said, "Don't chase food that rots, but chase food that will last forever. I, the Son of Man, give you this food from the Father."

They asked, "Tell us how we get it?"

Jesus replied, "The good work God requires is to believe in the One he sent."

Chase Jesus

Consider - John 6: 25 - 29

Jesus appears to be saying that chasing him is believing. Chase the truth of his words and the story of his life. This believing is the work the Father desires of us.

Here is the thing. Believing, in this case, was not just walking after or even following Jesus, because that is what the people did. They saw Jesus was special and wanted more, yet they really wanted him to provide their physical needs and fill their stomachs. They wanted Jesus on their own terms.

They followed him, but as you will see in the next entry when Jesus' request for commitment was stepped up, many of these following people walked away.

Jesus is asking for a belief that involves a chasing of him even through difficult teachings all the way to the cross… for the life of the world.

Chase Jesus. Believe.

Meditate

The crowd that chased Jesus around the lake acted like they were out for a stroll and just bumped into him asking, "Teacher, when did you arrive?"

Jesus saw through them and told them they were following him for free food and not to see the works of God he was doing.

Jesus said, "Don't chase food that rots, but chase food that will last forever. I, the Son of Man, give you this food from the Father."

They asked, "Tell us how we get it?"

Jesus replied, "The good work God requires is to believe in the One he sent."

Pray and Go

Twenty-four

Be still before God.
Exhale fully and let God fill you.

Meditate

Now Jesus' words get a little dicey.
He says, "It was actually the Father who gave our
people Manna-bread from heaven and not Moses.
Even then our people died in the desert. I am the
Real-True Bread delivered from God that gives life.

Come to me and you won't ever be hungry.

The Father wants everyone to look to me and
believe. They will have real life that never ends."

After this the people began to grumble. Jesus
continued, "Listen to the Father; learn from him. I
am the Bread that gives life. Eat me!
Eat this bread and you will never die.
Eat my flesh!
I give it for the life of the world."

For the Life of the World

Consider - John 6: 30 - 59

Jesus takes belief to the next level. He moves from chasing him to eating his flesh.

Here Jesus uses hyperbole to emphasis his point and also to foreshadow both the Last Supper and his death on the Cross. It was a hard teaching and it was obvious to the people listening that he wasn't promoting cannibalism, yet those were the words he used. Faith is hearing with our hearts and Jesus was looking for faith.

Later in the Last Supper, Jesus took the bread of the Passover dinner (this Jewish celebration of freedom), and said to the Twelve, "Eat, this bread is my flesh."

Jesus was inviting his true followers to receive him, take him in, and to follow in a selfless life of sacrifice that mirrored Jesus' life even to the point of death. Jesus' selflessness led him to the Cross.

Jesus gave his flesh… for the life of the world.

Jesus invites us to eat him and to live… for the life of the world and our neighbors.

Meditate

Now Jesus' words get a little dicey.
He says, "It was actually the Father who gave our
people Manna-bread from heaven and not Moses.
Even then our people died in the desert. I am the
Real-True Bread delivered from God that gives life.

Come to me and you won't ever be hungry.

The Father wants everyone to look to me and
believe. They will have real life that never ends."

After this the people began to grumble. Jesus
continued, "Listen to the Father; learn from him. I
am the Bread that gives life. Eat me!
Eat this bread and you will never die.
Eat my flesh!
I give it for the life of the world."

Pray and Go

Twenty-five

**Be still before God.
Exhale fully and let God fill you.**

Meditate

Jesus' words about his flesh being the real food they need to eat were too hard for these followers. Jesus said, "What if you see me, the Son of Man, rise back up into heaven to the place I came from!? Will you believe in me then? The Spirit of God gives life. My words are from the Spirit and they are Life."

Somehow Jesus knew which of his followers would believe and which ones would not. His followers are known by and enabled by the Father to believe.

Jesus' words were too hard to believe. Many from the crowd left. Jesus looked at his Twelve and said, "Do you want to leave too?"

Peter's reply was, "Who else should we follow? You have the words of Life, eternal life. We believe and know deep down that you are the Holy One promised by God."

Hard Words

Consider - John 6: 60 - 71

John the Writer was there when Jesus turned to the Twelve and asked if they also wished to leave. John and the Twelve were put on the spot. Jesus confused them and still they followed.

Would we have walked away? What kept them following Jesus?

John had just seen Jesus heal a paralyzed man, feed 5,000+ people, do a water walk and talk about bread in such a way that begged them to take him and eat the nourishment that gives life.

Even after witnessing the actions of Jesus, some of his words were hard to digest. The Twelve saw through these hard words and saw Jesus as the glimmer of hope for their broken souls.

God enables us. This is a promise of great hope. God works in us to give us the ability to believe in Jesus.

God enables us.

Peter found himself at a breaking point of frustration. I feel him saying, "I'd like to go away, but I have never experienced anyone like you! I see real life in you."

John the Writer was right there witnessing this frustration and the One that was unlike anyone who has ever existed.

Meditate

Jesus' words about his flesh being the real food they need to eat were too hard for these followers. Jesus said, "What if you see me, the Son of Man, rise back up into heaven to the place I came from!? Will you believe in me then? The Spirit of God gives life. My words are from the Spirit and they are Life."

Somehow Jesus knew which of his followers would believe and which ones would not. His followers are known by and enabled by the Father to believe.

Jesus' words were too hard to believe. Many from the crowd left. Jesus looked at his Twelve and said, "Do you want to leave too?"

Peter's reply was, "Who else should we follow? You have the words of Life, eternal life. We believe and know deep down that you are the Holy One promised by God."

Pray and Go

Twenty-six

Be still before God.
Exhale fully and let God fill you.

Meditate

Jesus remained in the Northern area of Galilee
where he grew up because in the South, Judea, some
wanted to kill him. It was not yet his time.

Living close to his family at this time, his not-yet-
believing brothers coaxed him,
"It's our Jewish Feast time, Jesus; if you want to be
famous, go to Jerusalem and show yourself to the
world."

Jesus told them it was not yet time.
Later Jesus went to Jerusalem in private.

People were asking around, "Where is Jesus?" Yet
some liked him and some did not.

Not yet time

Consider - John 7: 1 - 13

Consider the pain Jesus must have felt. He was the oldest of the brothers in his family, and the rest of his siblings, at least his brothers, did not believe his work or who he actually was.

Had Mary never told them the story of being visited by the Angel of God and his message of who her son was? Did she not tell them that Jesus was their half-brother? Did Jesus do no miracles until at the age of thirty when he changed water into wine? Was he only to them a sinless older brother who grew up and worked with wood?

In this story his brothers seemed to poke fun at him and maybe even show their doubt. Later we know at least one believed - James the Writer, who wrote the book of James.

Jesus was not wanted by his family at home or by the religious leaders in Jerusalem, and yet crowds of people still continued to chase him.

His time had not yet come... to die. He knew it was not yet time, but he was fully aware of why he came. He came to give his life... for the life of the world.

Jesus still had work to do.

Even today there is still work for us to do.

Meditate

Jesus remained in the Northern area of Galilee where he grew up because in the South, Judea, some wanted to kill him. It was not yet his time.

Living close to his family at this time, his not-yet-believing brothers coaxed him,
"It's our Jewish Feast time, Jesus; if you want to be famous, go to Jerusalem and show yourself to the world."

Jesus told them it was not yet time.
Later Jesus went to Jerusalem in private.

People were asking around, "Where is Jesus?" Yet some liked him and some did not.

Pray and Go

**Be still before God.
Exhale fully and let God fill you.**

Meditate

Jesus, knowing some wanted to kill him, still spoke at the Feast. They were amazed at his words. Jesus said, "I did not make this all up; my words come from the One who sent me. If anyone speaks his own words, it is only to honor himself. I speak the words God my Father gives me."

The religious leaders were trying to kill him because of his prior healing of the paralyzed man on the Sabbath day. Their understanding of the 'Law of Moses' trumped doing good.

Jesus' taught them, "Stop making judgments by what you see on the surface; listen and dig down deep for the true meaning, and then make the right judgments."

Listening Ear

Consider - John 7: 14 - 24

If we could hear all the words of Jesus even beyond what John the Writer recorded here, it would be amazing. The crowds were captivated and believed they had never heard words like this before.

Most of them had been to their temple because they were attending a religious feast. They heard their teachers before, but were amazed by Jesus. What he said was far different than the mere religious words that their teachers had spoken and lived out.

What was his secret? He tells us here. The words he spoke came directly from God our Father. Jesus was the listening-conduit of what the Father was saying to mankind.

This required a pure heart, humility of self and a listening ear.

It has been said that Christianity is a religion of many words. But are we carefully listening to Jesus?

Growing up we were taught not to tell others to "shut up." It is strong and rude language. However, a recent motto of mine has been to tell myself, "Just shut up and listen." My heart needs strong language at times.

May we have a listening ear.

May we listen carefully today to Jesus before we speak.

Meditate

Jesus, knowing some wanted to kill him, still spoke at the Feast. They were amazed at his words. Jesus said, "I did not make this all up, my words come from the One who sent me. If anyone speaks his own words, it is only to honor himself. I speak the words God my Father gives me."

The religious leaders were trying to kill him because of his prior healing of the paralyzed man on the Sabbath day. Their understanding of the 'Law of Moses' trumped doing good.

Jesus' taught them, "Stop making judgments by what you see on the surface, listen and dig down deep for the true meaning, and then make the right judgments."

Pray and Go

Be still before God.
Exhale fully and let God fill you.

Meditate

Even with the questions about Jesus many in the crowd put their faith in him saying, "What more miracles could we be looking for in anyone than what this man does? He looks like the Christ."

Jesus tells them he will only be with them a little while longer and then will go away. The place where he is heading to they cannot follow. The crowd listened but was confused.

Jesus speaks, "Anyone thirsty? Then come to me and drink of me.
Believe in me and springs of life will bubble from within and become overflowing rivers out of you."
By this he spoke of the coming Sacred-Spirit of God who would live inside of all who believe.

Overflowing Rivers

Consider - John 7: 25 - 44

Water is one of the continuing analogies that Jesus uses to teach us the work of God in us to the world (Isaiah 55 and John 4).

John the Writer traveled often with Jesus on foot on the dusty paths in the Ancient Middle East. My guess is that he had thirsty memories of those journeys. Jesus' words were opposite of what his mouth remembered.

Jesus asked if anyone was thirsty? John most likely said, "Yes." Then Jesus said, "Come to me", and John may have thought, "I did."

Then Jesus said, "Drink of me", and John might have remembered his turning water into wine.

We, like John, know thirst. It is a very basic and often-felt human need.

Jesus connected the drinking of his words to the life sustaining work of the Sacred Spirit of God inside us. It is as if we are sitting at the feet of Jesus with our ears open and Jesus is pouring life-water into our souls.

The waters don't stop there; they overflow out of us onto our neighbors... for others and for the life of the world.

Thirsty?

Meditate

Even with the questions about Jesus many in the crowd put their faith in him saying, "What more miracles could we be looking for in anyone than what this man does? He looks like the Christ."

Jesus tells them he will only be with them a little while longer and then will go away. The place where he is heading to they cannot follow. The crowd listened but was confused.

Jesus speaks, "Anyone thirsty? Then come to me and drink of me.
Believe in me and springs of life will bubble from within and become overflowing rivers out of you."
By this he spoke of the coming Holy Spirit who would live inside of all who believe.

Pray and Go

**Be still before God.
Exhale fully and let God fill you.**

Meditate

The crowd heard Jesus and they responded,
"He is the Great Prophet who was to come.
He is the promised Messiah, the Christ."
Still others had their doubts.

The Jewish guards from the temple reported all this
back to the religious leaders.
They were asked, "Why? Why didn't you arrest
Jesus?"

The guards replied, "We have never heard any man
ever speak like him."

Nick (from John 3), a religious leader, sticks up for
the Jewish legal process regarding hearing a man
before he is convicted.

His words are shot down by the rest of them.

Who is Jesus

Consider - John 7: 45 - 52

Everyone continues to try to figure out Jesus.

Their theology told them he was from the wrong place and wrong family. They did not know he was born in Bethlehem (as predicted) and his father was from the royal line of David (Matthew 1).

There religion was wrong. They saw Jesus doing good (on the Sabbath-rest day) and it did not fit into their law. Their religious rules blinded them. They could not understand the true heart of God.

Yet the common folk and the solders heard his message more clearly and saw something amazing in who he was. They believed he was special; they began to see him as the One promised to come and rescue. They lack the 'learning' of the leaders but knew what was 'real.'

This supports Jesus' words in the Sermon on the Mount in that the lowly, the mourners, the meek, and those hungry for what is right... would receive God's kingdom here on earth.

Who is Jesus?

Really, who is Jesus? It's possibly the single most important question one could ever tackle.

Continue to find John's Jesus. Seek him and listen.

Meditate

They crowd heard Jesus and they responded,
"He is the Great Prophet who was to come.
He is the promised Messiah, the Christ."
Still others had their doubts.

The Jewish guards from the temple reported all this
back to the religious leaders.
They were asked, "Why? Why didn't you arrest
Jesus?"

The guards replied, "We have never heard any man
ever speak like him."

Nicodemus (aka Nick from John 3), a religious
leader, sticks up for the Jewish legal process
regarding hearing a man before he is convicted.

His words are shot down by the rest of them.

Pray and Go

Thirty

Be still before God.
Exhale fully and let God fill you.

Meditate

At dawn the crowds surrounded Jesus in the temple courts. The religious guys wanted to trap him, so they threw in front of him and the crowd a woman caught in the act of adultery.

They made her stand there as if on trial and already condemned. "Jesus, she was caught in the act; Moses' Law says to stone her. What do you say?"

Jesus wrote with his finger in the dirt.
They continued to question him, so he stood and said, "If one of you has no sin please throw the first stone." He wrote in the dirt again.

They began to leave one by one, oldest to youngest.

Jesus asked the woman, "Where have all your condemners gone? I won't condemn you either. Go and leave your sinful life."

Grace is God's Fingerprint

Consider John 8: 1 - 11

They tried to trap Jesus by his character. They tried to trap him in his grace. Grace is the fingerprint of our God. Our fingerprint's confirm who we are.

They were trying to trap Jesus by asking him in public what they believed to be the overarching law. Their law condemns sinners. Jesus' identity was to offer grace. Grace is the law of God's Kingdom.

Grace throws no stones.

This is an amazing story that captures the contrasting heart of Jesus to the religious leaders. Their hearts where selfish, prideful and jealous of Jesus. They did not see people with God's eyes of grace but used people like pawns.

Here Jesus chose to not respond to their trap. It was not yet his time to die. Jesus, for whatever reason, wrote in the dirt. What did he write? Does the answer even matter? Obviously not or John would have recorded it.

John the Writer saw Jesus as a defender of the poor and the sinful. That is great news for us sinners. Jesus does not condemn her but does not approve of her behavior either in saying, "Go and leave your sinful life."

She must have been overwhelmed by his grace.

May we sinners drop the stones in our hands and live out the grace John saw in Jesus.

Meditate

At dawn the crowds surrounded Jesus in the temple courts. The religious guys wanted to trap him, so they threw in front of him and the crowd a woman caught in the act of adultery.

They made her stand there as if on trial and already condemned. "Jesus, she was caught in the act; Moses' Law says to stone her. What do you say?"

Jesus wrote with his finger in the dirt. They continued to question him so he stood and said, "If one of you has no sin please throw the first stone." He wrote in the dirt again.

They began to leave one by one, oldest to youngest.

Jesus asked the woman, "Where have all your condemners gone? I won't condemn you either. Go and leave your sinful life."

Pray and Go

Thirty-one

**Be still before God.
Exhale fully and let God fill you.**

Meditate

Jesus said, "I am the light in this world.

Anyone who follows me won't walk in the dark.

Their path will have the light necessary to live."

Light to live

Consider - John 8: 12

Consider these sentences of Jesus. He is dealing with the unbelief of some who are finding his teachings difficult, some religious leaders who are looking for ways to oust him, and leaders who just threw a woman caught in the act of sin under the bus.

Jesus brings out this powerful imagery of what he is in this world and what happens to those who follow him. He is light!

John the Writer quotes these words of Jesus that he also used in his summary of who Jesus is and was. John saw Jesus as his light. He saw Jesus as the only way forward in our dark world.

Jesus implies that the systems of this world are very dark. The world is broken and not running under the rules of God's Kingdom. Our separation from God is often not visible to us because this place is dark.

Imagine being in a sci-fi movie and living all your life underground with minimal light. You might have heard of the Sun, but have never seen it or realized the expanse of the brilliant light it possesses. Then one day you get above ground on a cloudless day and shield your eyes from the light. As your eyes adjust you begin to see things you had never seen before and life makes more sense.

Jesus is light in this world... he gives us light and the best way to move forward.

Meditate

Jesus said, "I am the light in this world.

Anyone who follows me won't walk in the dark.

Their path will have the light necessary to live."

Pray and Go

Thirty-two

Be still before God.
Exhale fully and let God fill you.

Meditate

"Jesus, your witness about yourself is not allowed. Where is your Father? Who in the world are you?" the religious leaders asked.

Jesus responded, "You judge people based on what humans see. I judge no one! I stand with the Father, and if I did judge, it would be a true verdict. You would know who the Father is if you knew me, and vice-versa.

You are a part of this world; I am part of another world. I will be going back there soon.

Believe in me, the Son of Man, or you will die condemned by your own sins. When you have lifted me up off of this earth, only then will you know that I am who I claim to be and that I do what my Father tells me."

I Judge no one

Consider - John 8: 13 - 30

Judgment and proof were what the religious leaders were looking for. They were attempting to judge the Son of God. They questioned him to prove he was a liar. Their minds were already made up.

They knew by his language that he referred to God the Father as his Father. This would make him the the Son of God. This was blasphemy in their eyes. They were trying to condemn him.

Jesus' words were profound and yet direct.

"I judge no one!" Looking back to John 3, Jesus told Nick that he did not come here to condemn anyone but to offer rescue to us all. John again points out that grace is the fingerprint of Jesus. Jesus wishes to save us.

We are also told elsewhere in Scripture that one day Jesus will judge mankind. Jesus has authority over us all, but for now he came to offer grace.

Jesus, walking on this earth, judged no one but came to rescue.

As he talked to his condemners, I seem to hear pain in his words as he offers them another chance to believe. He reminds them they, as we, are condemned by our own sins.

Then he gives his condemners a miracle to watch for... "when you see me lifted up on the Cross... and then I rise from death... you will know I am who I claim to be." Jesus continues to offer grace.

Meditate

"Jesus, your witness about yourself is not allowed. Where is your Father? Who in the world are you?" the religious leaders asked.

Jesus responded, "You judge people based on what humans see. I judge no one! I stand with the Father, and if I did judge, it would be a true verdict. You would know who the Father is if you knew me, and vice-versa.

You are a part of this world, I am part of another world. I will be going back there soon.

Believe in me, the Son of Man, or you will die condemned by your own sins. When you have lifted me up off of this earth, only then will you know that I am who I claim to be and that I do what my Father tells me."

Pray and Go

Thirty-three

Be still before God.
Exhale fully and let God fill you.

Meditate

"Do you want to be my followers? Hang on to each one of my words. This is how you know the truth. The truth frees you." Jesus spoke these words to the now-believing crowd.

They questioned Jesus further because they did not know they were slaves.

Jesus explained, "Anyone who sins is a slave to that sin. Slaves aren't a permanent part of a family. Children are always family. If I free you, you become free children of God.

You say God is your Father and yet you do not love me. That does not work. You do not hang on my words; this shows you are sons of the devil."

They grabbed stones to stone Jesus, but he slipped out of the temple.

Freedom

Consider - John 8: 31 - 59

What does it look like for us to be free from our sin and children of God? This passage gives some great insights into these two questions.

Jesus becomes brutally honest with the Jewish people who had begun to believe in him and then turned away. He talks about freedom; freedom to know what is true and freedom from the control of sin over us.

Followers of Jesus hang on his every word.

It is as if we are hanging onto the bottom of a bridge, and if we let go we would fall into a deep ravine. Holding on to the teachings of Jesus sets us free. Makes us alive. Helps us see what is real and good. Then we are free to love everyone… both our self, our neighbor and any enemy.

The second part is that the sin in our lives traps us and enslaves us. Our desire to be liked or our fears can force us to sin, hold us down and enslave us. Many of the things we want in this dark world entice us and control us when Jesus is all that we need.

Jesus invites everyone to hang onto his words and become the free children of God. We were designed to be free to live out the Kingdom of God… Jesus offers this to us again.

Freedom comes through Jesus.

Meditate

"Do you want to be my followers? Hang on to each one of my words. This is how you know the truth. The truth frees you." Jesus spoke these words to the now-believing crowd.

They questioned Jesus further because they did not know they were slaves.

Jesus explained, "Anyone who sins is a slave to that sin. Slaves aren't a permanent part of a family. Children are always family. If I free you, you become free children of God.

You say God is your Father and yet you do not love me. That does not work. You do not hang on my words; this shows you are sons of the devil."

They grabbed stones to stone Jesus, but he slipped out of the temple.

Pray and Go

Thirty-four

Be still before God.
Exhale fully and let God fill you.

Meditate

Walking, Jesus and the Twelve saw a blind man. The Twelve asked Jesus, "We heard he was blind from birth, so who sinned?"

Jesus explained, "No one! The sin was not brought on because of one man's sin, but to show God's work in this man. I am light to this world. I'm still shining and working. Believe me, night is coming soon."

Jesus spit! Yes, Jesus spit on the ground and made mud salve. After he put it on the man's eyes, he sent him to wash in the pool called 'Sent.'

He was healed and went home. His neighbors were bewildered and amazed. "Who did this?" they asked. He replied, "It was Jesus."

The Light Loves Mercy

Consider - John 9: 1 - 12

Light walks up to a blind man and opens his eyes. Jesus restores this man's sight to help him see the Light of the world. The Light continues to shine.

The Twelve and their culture assumed punishment from God if something bad happened to someone. Possibly that is somewhere in our nature. They/we assumed a God craving immediate judgment, but Jesus knew his Father longing to show mercy. We are told in Scripture the character of God is to be "slow to anger" and that he loves to show mercy.

This man's blindness was to show God to him and to the world. The Light loves mercy.

Jesus did not have to stop on his journey to heal this man, but since he is always working and doing the mercy-work of the Father, he stopped and restored the sight of this blind man. John the Writer continues to show us that the character of Jesus is mercy. His actions are the light we need.

Insects fly toward the light at night. (And sometimes a bug zapper.) The light is magnetic. The crowds found Jesus' words and actions were magnetic.

Why did Jesus spit and make mud instead of just speak a word? Who knows. We are not told. Possibly it was to see if the man would practice faith and actually follow-through with the words of Jesus for him to wash in the pool. He was 'sent' in faith to a pool whose name meant 'Sent.' Faith brings his sight. The Light loves mercy.

Meditate

Walking, Jesus and the Twelve saw a blind man. The Twelve asked Jesus, "We heard he was blind from birth, so who sinned?"

Jesus explained, "No one! The sin was not brought on because of one man's sin, but to show God's work in this man. I am light to this world. I'm still shining and working. Believe me, night is coming soon."

Jesus spit! Yes, Jesus spit on the ground and made mud salve. After he put it on the man's eyes, he sent him to wash in the pool called 'Sent.'

He was healed and went home. His neighbors were bewildered and amazed. "Who did this?" they asked. He replied, "It was Jesus."

Pray and Go

Thirty-five

Be still before God.
Exhale fully and let God fill you.

Meditate

The Jewish leaders were divided over Jesus' miracle. Some said, "He's not from God because he works/ heals on the Sabbath-Rest Day," yet some said, "Sinners can't do things like making a man see!"

Confused. Hardhearted. They questioned the former blind man and his parents about Jesus. Then they summoned the man to them a second time for questioning and said, "Give glory to God, not this man named Jesus, for he is a sinner."

Frustrated, the man responded, "I don't know about that. This I know. I was blind, and now I see clearly. You continue to ask me about him; do you want to be one of his followers too?!"

Angry, they tossed him out of the synagogue where all are welcome by God to worship.

Jesus, Not in a Box

Consider - John 9: 13 - 34

Why do we try to figure out all the mysteries of our God? We try to make him understandable. We try to put the all-powerful and all-knowing God into our rules and our terms. Is this faith or control? Jesus, the Son of God, could not fit into their box.

The religious Jewish leaders continually found Jesus not lining up to their thinking. Their hearts and their thinking needed to change to embrace our mysterious God.

When confronted with Jesus, our ways need to change, not God's. John the Writer knew this to be true. He witnessed Jesus breaking many of the religious rules. He discovered in this miracle that mercy trumps religious rules. He saw the heart of God as continually wanting to bless others no matter what their circumstances were.

This man witnessed God's mercy in Jesus' actions. In the religious leaders' theology, Jesus' actions did not make sense because they held their rules above the greatest commandment of loving God with everything and loving your neighbor as yourself.

In the beginning of this miracle, Jesus told the Twelve he was doing this to show God to this man and through this man. We can tell by the former blind man's words that he was beginning to see God in the light of Jesus. Faith sees.

Faith does not come by our religion but in looking to Jesus. Jesus is way beyond our religious boxes.

Meditate

The Jewish leaders were divided over Jesus' miracle. Some said, "He's not from God because he works/heals on the Sabbath-Rest Day;" yet some said, "Sinners can't do things like making a man see!"

Confused. Hardhearted. They questioned the former blind man and his parents about Jesus. Then they summoned the man to them a second time for questioning and said, "Give glory to God, not this man named Jesus, for he is a sinner."

Frustrated, the man responded, "I don't know about that. This I know. I was blind, and now I see clearly. You continue to ask me about him, do you want to be one of his followers too?"

Angry, they tossed him out of the synagogue where all are welcome by God to worship.

Pray and Go

Thirty-six

Be still before God.
Exhale fully and let God fill you.

Meditate

The religious leaders threw the newly-seeing man out of God's house, but Jesus went and found him to restore him.

Jesus asked him, "Do you believe in the Son of Man?"

"Tell me and I will." the man replied.

Jesus responded, "You are speaking with him now."

The man fell to his knees and worshiped Jesus saying, "Master, I believe."

Jesus then adds, "I've come so the blind will see, and those who think they already see will be blind."

The religious leaders took his words personally knowing Jesus was calling them blind.

Seeing

Consider - John 9: 35 - 41

Here Jesus uses the life of this man and confronts us with the question, "What does it mean to see?"

In this story the newly-seeing man reveals the spiritual blindness of the religious who are following God on their own terms and with their own formulas.

They excluded this man from the place of worship of their God. Jesus includes him back into relationship with him. He sought him out to restore him.

Seeing God requires faith. Remember in chapter six after the Twelve had witnessed Jesus feeding the 5,000 and walking on the water, some of them thought about leaving. Yet something pulled them back. Although they did not understand his difficult teachings, they knew deep in their hearts that Jesus had the words of never-ending life.

Seeing faith does not have all the answers but looks to Jesus. Seeing faith is open for God's Sacred Spirit to give life.

Imagine being this man and first handedly knowing darkness your entire life only to meet Jesus, the Light of the world, washing and seeing for the first time. Then Jesus asks his heart to see and it does. May this be true spiritually in our own lives.

John the Writer may have witnessed this miracle and joined in worship with this new follower of Jesus. See Jesus.

Meditate

The religious leaders threw the newly-seeing man out of God's house, but Jesus went and found him to restore him.

Jesus asked him, "Do you believe in the Son of Man?"

"Tell me and I will," the man replied.

Jesus responded, "You are speaking with him now."

The man fell to his knees and worshiped Jesus saying, "Master, I believe."

Jesus then adds, "I've come so the blind will see, and those who think they already see will be blind."

The religious leaders took his words personally knowing Jesus was calling them blind.

Pray and Go

Thirty-seven

Be still before God.
Exhale fully and let God fill you.

Meditate

"There are many sheep in the sheep pen and men have different intentions for them. Thieves jump the fence to steal some, but the shepherd walks right through the gate.

The shepherd calls out to his sheep by name. He calls in his native tongue, and they hear, follow and are led out of the gate. The rest remain in the pen.

The shepherd goes in front of the sheep; the sheep follow because they know his voice."

Jesus then added, "I am the Good Shepherd and the good shepherd lays down his life for his sheep. When the wolves attack, the part-timers run away, but I lay down my life for my sheep.

The Father loves me because I lay down my life."

I lay down my life

Consider John 10: 1 - 21

This parable of Jesus reveals his sacrificing heart for us. The shepherd, we are told, leads the sheep out of the pen. Although some safety resides in the pen, the sheep must leave the pen to find food and water. The shepherd calls his sheep out of the pen for their benefit.

These sheep won't just follow any shepherd. The sheep know the voice of their shepherd and follow that shepherd because they know he takes care of them. A prior relationship is implied.

Not every sheep comes out of the pen, only the ones who listen carefully. They listen carefully for their name to be called by the voice they recognize, the one who has a proven track record.

Then Jesus takes the livestock parable to a new level. Five times in this passage Jesus tells the people listening that he, the Good Shepherd, will lay down his life for his sheep.

I wonder at which of the five times in the story did the people finally hear that Jesus would die for the life of his sheep… for the life of the world.

This parable parallels the famous Psalm 23 that many in the crowd would have known well. "The Lord is my shepherd…"

John the Writer later saw Jesus, the Good Shepherd, as the one who did lay down his life for his sheep.

Meditate

"There are many sheep in the sheep pen. and men have different intentions for them. Thieves jump the fence to steal some, but the shepherd walks right through the gate.

The shepherd calls out to his sheep by name. He calls in his native tongue and they hear, follow and are led out of the gate. The rest remain in the pen.

The shepherd goes in front of the sheep; the sheep follow because they know his voice."

Jesus then added, "I am the Good Shepherd and the good shepherd lays down his life for his sheep. When the wolves attack, the part-timers run away, but I lay down my life for my sheep.

The Father loves me because I lay down my life."

Pray and Go

Thirty-eight

Be still before God.
Exhale fully and let God fill you.

Meditate

In the middle of Jesus' parable he told to his Jewish
sisters and brothers about the sheep and the Good
Shepherd he said this:

"You are not my only sheep.
I have sheep that aren't even from your pen.
I will bring them along with us.
These sheep will listen carefully to my voice.
I will gather them together with you;
you will all be one flock,
and you will all have me as your One Good
Shepherd."

A Gathering

Consider - John 10: 16

Throughout the story of God and his people through the whole Old Testament God is gathering his people to himself. We have a God who desires to be with us.

Although our Good Shepherd stands with open arms wishing to gather us all, our sinful hearts chase other things we think will bring us happiness. He sees us as his sheep, the sheep he longs to lead and gather.

In the Old Testament the blessing of a gathering and restoration was promised to a man named Abraham, the father of the Jewish people and the father of faith. This promise of God was to bless his seed or offspring in Genesis 22. We are told in the New Testament that Jesus was the seed of Abraham who came to bless the whole world. The plan was for Abraham's people to follow their God and experience so much blessing that the world would rush toward this blessing and gather in the worship of God. Their sin kept this from happening, so Jesus came to gather the nations through the shedding of his blood.

The Jewish people who followed were the first sheep in Jesus' parable. We who follow Jesus are the adopted sheep into this large flock .

Listen carefully for Jesus' voice.

Follow our One Shepherd.

Enjoy the "baaahhh's" from many different kind of sheep that God is gathering with us.

Meditate

In the middle of Jesus' parable he told to his Jewish sisters and brothers about the sheep and the Good Shepherd he said this:

"You are not my only sheep.
I have sheep that aren't even from your pen.
I will bring them along with us.
These sheep will listen carefully to my voice.
I will gather them together with you;
you will all be one flock,
and you will all have me as your One Good Shepherd."

Pray and Go

Thirty-nine

Be still before God.
Exhale fully and let God fill you.

Meditate

The Jewish leaders told Jesus directly, "If you are saying you are the Christ/Messiah, tell us."

Jesus replied, "I have already, and you did not believe me. My Father-generated-miracles answer your question. You can't see it because you are not my sheep!

My flock of sheep hear my voice; they know me; I know them; they follow me, and
I give them life that never ends.
No one anywhere can ever rip them from my grasp.
No one anywhere can ever rip them from my Father's grasp.
My Father and I are One."

Then they grabbed stones to kill Jesus.

God's Grasp

Consider - John 10: 22 - 33

Jesus went back to Jerusalem for the celebration of Hanukkah, the Jewish celebration of Jerusalem being given back to them by an Assyrian ruler. At that time they restored the Second Temple. This was about 200 years before Jesus came to earth.

Jesus is confronted again and continues to talk about sheep. John the Writer devotes a good bit of his writings to sheep. Here John records more detail for us sheep.

God's hand and God's grasp.

In our world it may feel at times as if something else is holding us, or someone else is gripping us. Here Jesus reminds his sheep to listen for his voice continually, to believe we are fully known by Jesus, to keep moving and following him. We no longer need to fear the promise of death that hangs over mortal human beings because of sin in the Garden of Eden.

It is as if Jesus' sheep are immortal. But why is this so?

Jesus grasps and holds his sheep ... and never lets go. God the Father doubly grasps and holds us in his offer of love. Picture God holding us is the way a shepherd would pick up a sheep with both hands and hold it closely to his chest.

Know today, know the security and protection of being held in God's grasp... forever.

Meditate

The Jewish leaders told Jesus directly, "If you are
saying you are the Christ/Messiah tell us."

Jesus replied, "I have already, and you did not
believe me. My Father-generated-miracles answer
your question. You can't see it because you are not
my sheep!

My flock of sheep hear my voice; they know me; I
know them; they follow me, and
I give them life that never ends.
No one anywhere can ever rip them from my grasp.
No one anywhere can ever rip them from my
Father's grasp.
My Father and I are One."

Then they grabbed stones to kill Jesus.

Pray and Go

Forty

Be still before God.
Exhale fully and let God fill you.

Meditate

"We are going to stone you; you say you are God!"
the Jewish leaders said.

Jesus replied, "In your own Law, in a Psalm, God
says, "I say you are 'gods.'

Now if God said this, how can you stone me for
that? The Scripture is always true,
especially the promise of the One God sent into the
world. Why accuse me? Look again at your
Scriptures. Look again at my miracles. They are from
the Father."

The leaders again tried to stone him, but Jesus
escaped.

God's offspring

Consider - John 10: 33 - 42, Psalm 82

These are very confusing but super cool words of Jesus. He affirms the words God spoke through David in Psalm 82 calling men 'gods.' Then Jesus insists that they wanted to kill him for something God said was true.

David wrote Psalm 82 using very harsh words about Israel's leaders. They were wicked leaders. These leaders showed favor to and defended other evil people. They avoided defending the fatherless and the weak, so God through David tells them to uphold justice for the oppressed and the poor. These leaders were stumbling in darkness, and their sins shook the very core of the earth.

Then God encourages them saying, "You are gods."

It seems God is saying that people are the offspring of God, therefore, sons of God, and yet their behavior rocked the very core of the earth. We are create in God's image,… to image our God.

Jesus' words offend them on several levels since they most likely knew this Psalm. He showed them they did not know the Scriptures. He showed them that God looks down and sees all men as his offspring and potential image-bearers. He compares these leaders to leaders of old who did not defend the fatherless, weak, oppressed and the poor.

The Father and His Son see their behavior as rocking the very core of this good earth when they/we were created to act like our God. The true offspring of God behave like their Father.

Meditate

"We are going to stone you; you say you are God!"
the Jewish leaders said.

Jesus replied, "In your own Law, in a Psalm, God
says, "I say you are 'gods.'

Now if God said this, how can you stone me for
that. The Scripture is always true,
especially the promise of the One God sent into the
world. Why accuse me? Look again at your
Scriptures. Look again at my miracles. They are from
the Father."

The leaders again tried to stone him, but Jesus
escaped.

Pray and Go

Be still before God.
Exhale fully and let God fill you.

Meditate

Jesus' good friend Lazarus was dying. The message was sent to Jesus, "Master, the one you love is sick."

Jesus predicted the outcome of Lazarus' sickness to the Twelve. "Lazarus' sickness is for God's glory and won't end in death. Through his sickness God's Son will receive glory."

After staying two more days, they left for the region of Judea which was two miles from Jerusalem. The men there wanted to kill Jesus. A courageous Thomas said, "We too will go with Jesus and die with him."

Jesus told the Twelve his friend was sleeping, meaning he was now dead. The Twelve did not understand. Then Jesus said, "Let's go."

God's Timing

Consider - John 11: 1 - 16

Jesus was not operating on his own clock or his own schedule. John records this story and Jesus' words to show the bravery of Jesus, knowing the Father's timing as he began to march toward his coming death.

Jesus delays his trip to Lazarus' home to give him time to die. Yes, Jesus could have gone earlier and healed him. Jesus, the One who offers us life, paused and waited. During this pause he told the Twelve the end result would not be his friend's death. The end result would ultimately show people he was God, for only God gives life.

This is just one more story where someone felt that Jesus loved them. Lazarus' two sisters described their brother to Jesus as the one he loved.

This story is all about God's timing. For Lazarus and his two sisters, Martha and Mary, Jesus' timing was too late. For God it was just on time. This story sets up Jesus' final week before his death in what has been called, "the Passion week of Christ." Jesus' ultimate glorification followed his own death. His coming resurrection showed all who he was.

God's timing is perfect even in our own lives. Things may seem difficult now, but God is perfecting you in the same way the book of Hebrews tells us that even Jesus was "perfected in his suffering."

It was now time for Jesus to march toward Jerusalem and his own death. Courageous Thomas also saw it coming and said bring it on.

Meditate

Jesus' good friend Lazarus was dying. The message was sent to Jesus, "Master, the one you love is sick."

Jesus predicted the outcome of Lazarus' sickness to the Twelve. "Lazarus' sickness is for God's glory and won't end in death. Through his sickness God's Son will receive glory."

After staying two more days they left for the region of Judea, which was two miles from Jerusalem. The men there wanted to kill Jesus. A courageous Thomas said, "We too will go with Jesus and die with him."

Jesus told the Twelve his friend was sleeping, meaning he was now dead. The Twelve did not understand, then Jesus said, "Let's go."

Pray and Go

**Be still before God.
Exhale fully and let God fill you.**

Meditate

As they approach, Martha, Lazarus' sister, runs out to meet Jesus. She said, "Master, if you were here he would still live. But I have confidence God will still do what you ask him."

Jesus said, "Lazarus will rise again, ...and not just in the last days. I am Resurrection and I am Life; anyone who believes in me will live, even if he dies."

Martha responded, "Yes. I believe you are the Christ/Messiah, the very Son of God sent to us."

Mary, Lazarus' other sister, came to Jesus weeping and saying, "If you had been here he would still be alive." The mourners behind her also came out of the town weeping.

LIFE

Life is in Him

Consider - John 11: 17 - 32

In this account we see the two sisters running out to Jesus, and by their words we can see their faith in him. Jesus was not only their friend but also their Savior. Martha and then Mary ran to Jesus in their grief.

Jesus was Resurrection and Jesus was life. The faithful Jewish people knew the promise of their people someday rising out of the grave. This was the resurrection of the dead, and Jesus was the means for this coming back to life.

Here we see in Jesus' words that he is Life. Jesus was with the Father when this world was breathed into existence, and he breathes life again into his followers.

Martha believed it; Mary believed it; and in the next section so will the crowd after they witness a resurrection of someone who was dead.

Jesus is Life. Life is in him.

Martha knew of 'the last days,' or the coming day of God to bring back to life his people on the earth. The resurrection is not reincarnation or a ghostly returning of the spirit, but a day when our physical bodies with rise out of the earth to life… again.

Jesus said, "I am Resurrection and I am Life; anyone who believes in me will live, even if he dies."

Life is in Jesus.

Meditate

As they approach, Martha, Lazarus' sister, runs out to meet Jesus. She said, "Master, if you were here he would still live. But I have confidence God will still do what you ask him."

Jesus said, "Lazarus will rise again, …and not just in the last days. I am Resurrection and I am Life, anyone who believes in me will live, even if he dies."

Martha responded, "Yes. I believe you are the Christ/Messiah, the very Son of God sent to us."

Mary, Lazarus' other sister, came to Jesus weeping and saying, "If you had been here he would still be alive." The mourners behind her also came out of the town weeping.

Pray and Go

Forty-three

Be still before God.
Exhale fully and let God fill you.

Meditate

Jesus, becoming emotionally troubled, asked them, "Where is Lazarus' tomb?" Jesus sobbed.

The crowd said, "It is so obvious how much he loved Lazarus." Others said, "He healed many people; couldn't he have stopped him from dying?"

Arriving at the tomb, Jesus told them to remove the stone. Martha objected saying, "It's been four days and his body stinks."

Jesus reminds her that he told her to believe… to see God's glory.

Jesus prayed aloud, "Father, thank you for always hearing me and hearing me now so these mourners will believe you sent me."

"Lazarus, come out!" And he did!

Jesus sobbed

Consider - John 11: 33 - 44

Jesus is deeply moved by hurting people. He knew what he was going to do, and yet he felt the deep pain of Martha, Mary, their friends and family who came together to grieve their loss.

Jesus sobbed. God loves us.

This wasn't just the wiping of the eye. Jesus sobbed. Some versions of Scripture say he wept.

Jesus sobs with humanity in our grief. Yet his grieving is not without hope. Jesus sees the end of the story. Soon he would go to the Cross to bear our sickness, carry our sorrows and be pierced by our sin. Jesus is Resurrection and Life, he is also Victory and Hope.

Now it was time. He brought Lazarus back to life. This started the clock ticking toward his death in the coming week. Lazarus' great miracle was the last straw for the Jewish leaders who could not believe. Lazarus' restored life would lead to Jesus' death.

This miracle was a picture of what Jesus was about to do. If the religious leaders kill Jesus, could he be his own Resurrection?

The people knew Jesus as a great Miracle Worker and now they saw him as God. Only God gives life.

Jesus sobs with humanity and then does something about it.

Meditate

Jesus, becoming emotionally troubled, asked them, "Where is Lazarus' tomb?" Jesus sobbed.

The crowd said, "It is so obvious how much he loved Lazarus." Others said, "He healed many people; couldn't he have stopped him from dying?"

Arriving at the tomb, Jesus told them to remove the stone. Martha objected saying, "It's been four days and his body stinks."

Jesus reminds her that he told her to believe… to see God's glory.

Jesus prayed aloud, "Father, thank you for always hearing me and hearing me now so these mourners will believe you sent me."

"Lazarus, come out!" And he did!

Pray and Go

**Be still before God.
Exhale fully and let God fill you.**

Meditate

Some believed in Jesus and some did not. Word about this miracle got back to Jerusalem and the Jewish leaders set out to stop Jesus.

One of the prominent leaders, Caiaphas, had prophesied that very year that Jesus would die for the Jewish nation and the children of God around the world. Then Jesus would make both groups one.

Caiaphas told the other leaders, "You don't get it. It is best to let him die for the nation; it is better than the whole nation dying."

They together set out to kill Jesus.

One to Die for Any

Consider - John 11: 45 - 57

It is super interesting that this leader, Caiaphas, had actually prophesied that Jesus would die for their nation and for God's children around the world. His prophecy was true.

Although killing the Son of God was not a godly act, he must have heard this message from God of what the Father was doing in the world. In the Old Testament God uses evil rulers to carry out his will.

God's plan can include us but is far bigger than us living it out with perfection. God was accomplishing his will in the world in his time through religious leaders who were all messed up, … because now was the time for Jesus.

God had promised to Adam, Abraham, Moses, David, Isaiah and Jeremiah through the lines of Abraham and then David, that One would come to offer rescue to their people and for the life of the world.

Caiaphas' words were the fulfillment of this promise about the work of the Messiah, Anointed One, or the Christ.

God's promise was to everyone who would look to Jesus, the Messiah, and believe.

Jesus was the one to die for anyone who would believe.

Meditate

Some believed in Jesus and some did not. Word about this miracle got back to Jerusalem and the Jewish leaders set out to stop Jesus.

One of the prominent leaders, Caiaphas, had prophesied that very year that Jesus would die for the Jewish nation and the children of God around the world. Then Jesus would make both groups one.

Caiaphas told the other leaders, "You don't get it. It is best to let him die for the nation; it is better than the whole nation dying."

Together they set out to kill Jesus.

Pray and Go

Forty-five

Be still before God.
Exhale fully and let God fill you.

Meditate

Countdown to the Passover celebration. Six more days. Jesus arrived back in Lazarus' hometown, and Martha and Mary threw a dinner celebrating Jesus.

Martha served and Mary took her large bottle of perfume and poured it all over Jesus' feet. As she did this she wiped his feet with her hair.

The beautiful smell filled the room.

Here is a little insight into Judas' heart. Judas complained about the waste, saying it should have been sold and the money given to the poor. He knew how to play the game, but he sometimes stole money given to support Jesus' work.

Jesus knew his heart and said, "I won't be here long. Her actions are to prep my body for burial, so let her alone."

Beautiful Response

Consider - John 12: 1 - 11

This was a beautiful act of adoring Jesus. It appears Mary did this because of the goodness he showed her family in bringing her brother back to life. The larger reason of God was to prepare Jesus for a quick pre-Sabbath burial.

Martha served the food while Mary spontaneously, passionately and creatively also brought her best to Jesus.

Imagine for a moment how you might repay someone who just brought your sibling back to life. Wouldn't you offer the most valuable thing you have? Wouldn't you do almost anything for them?

Mary adored and celebrated Jesus in a very raw and genuine love response of her soul. This was a beautiful act of pure worship. It was a beautiful response to the rescue Jesus gave them. Life over death.

Judas responded a very different way... in criticism and selfishness. John writes this story in such a way that begs a response to Jesus. Does our heart respond in a passionate and spontaneous way to the love of Jesus, or in criticism and selfishness toward others?

May we respond today to Jesus and to others out of the goodness he has shown us.

Meditate

Countdown to the Passover celebration. Six more days. Jesus arrived back in Lazarus' hometown and Martha and Mary threw a dinner celebrating Jesus.

Martha served and Mary took her large bottle of perfume and poured it all over Jesus' feet. As she did this she wiped his feet with her hair.

The beautiful smell filled the room.

Here is a little insight into Judas' heart. Judas complained about the waste, saying it should have been sold and the money given to the poor. He knew how to play the game, but he sometimes stole money given to support Jesus' work.

Jesus knew his heart and said, "I won't be here long. Her actions are to prep my body for burial, so let her alone."

Pray and Go

Forty-six

Be still before God.
Exhale fully and let God fill you.

Meditate

The following day the crowd in Jerusalem heard
Jesus was coming… they grabbed palm limbs and
sprinted out to meet Jesus.

They found Jesus slowly and humbly riding toward
town on a young donkey.

They cried out praises from their Scriptures,
"Save! You are blessed, the One coming in the name
of the Lord God.
You are blessed, the King of Israel."
They repeated it over and over.

The crowds knew it to be true, the disciples were
unaware of the prophesy, and the Jewish leaders
lamented, "This is not helping. The entire world is
running to Jesus."

Running to Jesus

Consider - John 12: 12 - 19

The stage was now set by God; the crowd ran to Jesus like animals to their feed. The raising of Lazarus in the town just outside the large city of Jerusalem caused a ripple effect.

The word was out and people ran to Jesus to be "saved." They were looking for salvation personally and for their nation.

John the Writer records this powerful account of the humble Jesus. With such fame he could have chosen to enter and take Jerusalem in power. Jesus instead rode in humility on a young donkey. This is the kind of scene we visualize of his young mother Mary riding on during her pregnancy.

A young donkey was still learning life and learning to be ridden. Donkeys are methodical and slow. Jesus sits on this donkey in what has been called the "triumphal entry" but what is more like seeing a friend come home after a tiring journey. He looks gentle and lowly, fully aware he is riding toward his death.

The crowd cried out the kingly praises of rescue from Psalm 118. A psalm that begins and ends with the praises, "God's love lasts forever." The Crowd cried out, "Save!" They believed God was now here and saw his love lasting forever.

Meditate

The following day the crowd in Jerusalem heard
Jesus was coming… they grabbed palm limbs and
sprinted out to meet Jesus.

They found Jesus slowly and humbly riding toward
town on a young donkey.

They cried out praises from their Scriptures,
"Save! You are blessed, the One coming in the name
of the Lord God.
You are blessed, the King of Israel."
They repeated it over and over.

The crowds knew it to be true, the disciples were
unaware of the prophesy, and the Jewish leaders
lamented, "This is not helping. The entire world is
running to Jesus."

Pray and Go

**Be still before God.
Exhale fully and let God fill you.**

Meditate

News of Jesus spread beyond the Jewish people, and now some Greek people sought him out too.

Jesus was again assured it was now his time so he spoke these words,
"A kernel of wheat must fall to the ground and then die in the earth to produce more wheat.

The person who loves his own life above others will lose his life. The one who places his life second to others will never lose his life. Never!

Anyone who serves me must follow me. That servant will be with me and will be honored by the Father."

Kernel of wheat

Consider - John 12: 20 - 26

Jesus was affirmed that his time to leave the earth was near because people beyond his Jewish world were seeking him out. His message was going out to the whole world.

In this short parable Jesus puts to words what his life has been all about. His life is like a kernel of wheat. When a kernel of wheat is on the stalk it is just one seed. It can be cut down and eaten, which only fills one person. When it drops off the stalk and dies in the ground, other wheat stalks grow out of that one seed and the wheat crop can go on and on, continuing and filling many people.

Jesus' life through his death would produce fruits now for 2,000 plus years.

Secondly, Jesus tells them that if you live your life for yourself, then that is precisely what your life was lived for… yourself. However, if we place our wants second behind the wants of others, then we will have life now and never-ending.

John the Writer saw this short parable lived out before him over the three years he lived with Jesus. I wonder if he viewed Jesus on the Cross as wheat dying or if the trauma of the whole event was too much for him.

Following Jesus in this way comes with the great promise of having real-life here and never losing it.

May we die today to our wants and live second behind the needs of others.

Meditate

News of Jesus spread beyond the Jewish people and now some Greek people sought him out too.

Jesus was again assured it was now his time so he spoke these words,
"A kernel of wheat must fall to the ground and then die in the earth to produce more wheat.

The person who loves his own life above others will lose his life. The one who places his life second to others will never lose his life. Never!

Anyone who serves me must follow me. That servant will be with me and will be honored by the Father."

Pray and Go

Forty-eight

Be still before God.
Exhale fully and let God fill you.

Meditate

Jesus continues his talk, "Right now my heart carries a heavy burden. Should I ask the Father to save me now? No, this burden is why I came. Bring glory to yourself, Father, in me."

God bellowed from heaven, "I have and I will." Some thought this voice was thunder and some said it was an angel.

Jesus said, "Now is judgment time. Now the prince of this place will be driven from this place. My being lifted up will draw all people to me."

He spoke of being lifted up to explain his coming death, but the crowd was confused.

"I am Light to this dark place and won't be here long; put your trust in the Light," added Jesus.

A Heavy Burden

Consider - John 12: 27 - 36

Jesus, the Son of God, carried a heavy burden. He took on the power and the systems of this dark world.

To do this he would offer his body up in a painful and predicted way of death. Jesus, the Light, was carrying a painful and a heavy burden.

Yet God the Father was accomplishing great glory in his Son and through his Son in what would follow. Jesus knew it would cost him much.

It was as if two heavyweight fighters were stepping into the ring and one fighter, Light, would offer to the other, Darkness, free punches for a whole round with his arms out to his side.

Jesus was taking the punches, but the Father had a plan. A plan allowing the swinging fighter, Darkness, to do exactly what he wanted to not knowing that it would only destroy himself.

Jesus took the punches and carried a heavy burden. His being knocked to the ground would lead to ultimate victory.

We are standing at ringside, and Jesus asks us to trust in the Light. Trust in the grace he is offering us. Trust even though it does not make sense in this dark place.

Jesus is fighting for us. Trust in the Light.

Meditate

Jesus continues his talk, "Right now my heart carries a heavy burden. Should I ask the Father to save me now? No, this burden is why I came. Bring glory to yourself, Father, in me."

God bellowed from heaven, "I have and I will." Some thought this voice was thunder and some said it was an angel.

Jesus said, "Now is judgment time. Now the prince of this place will be driven from this place. My being lifted up will draw all people to me."

He spoke of being lifted up to explain his coming death, but the crowd was confused.

"I am Light to this dark place and won't be here long; put your trust in the Light." added Jesus.

Pray and Go

Forty-nine

Be still before God.
Exhale fully and let God fill you.

Meditate

Unbelief continued in the crowd. This was predicted
by the prophet Isaiah when he said,
"Lord, who will believe and know your strong arms?

For a time... those who are blind with dead hearts
and living in sin... will not be able to see God,
process his truth, or turn back to him. If they would,
they would be healed."

Isaiah spoke these words foreseeing Jesus' coming
and his glory.

Some of the leaders did believe, but they would not
speak it in fear of being kicked out of the
synagogue. They loved people's praise more than
God's praise.

Sight?

Consider - John 12: 37 - 43

What is sight? These people saw and heard God standing right in front of them and still could not see him. They were blinded.

The section John quotes is from Isaiah 6. In this vision of Isaiah the Lord stood right in front of him and Isaiah heard God speak. The Lord spoke these words about a time of blindness of his people who were locked in the darkness of their sin.

Spiritual blindness can happen gradually. I personally have later looked back and seen this in my own life. In those times my faith journey becomes all about carving out my own selfish life and not about responding to God's love with a grateful heart. Unaware of my blindness, I lose sight of Jesus and forget that my day should be about him and others. As I spiral into a deeper darkness, I judge people more freely, have more opinions that I share and lose focus of the greatest commandment to love God with everything and love my neighbor in the way I love myself.

Blindness has now set in. Apart from the intervention of Jesus in my life, I can never re-see the Light, or even pursue Jesus who gives me life.

John the Writer records this deep darkness in the crowd and in the same moment saw the glory of God himself walking on the earth in front of them.

Jesus is the Light, the sight of the world. May we look to Jesus today to see.

Meditate

Unbelief continued in the crowd. This was predicted
by the prophet Isaiah when he said,
"Lord, who will believe and know your strong arms?

For a time… those who are blind with dead hearts
and living in sin… will not be able to see God,
process his truth, or turn back to him. If they would
they would be healed."

Isaiah spoke these words foreseeing Jesus' coming
and his glory.

Some of the leaders did believe, but they would not
speak it in fear of being kicked out of the
synagogue. They loved people's praise more than
God's praise.

Pray and Go

Fifty

Be still before God.
Exhale fully and let God fill you.

Meditate

Jesus shouted to the crowd, "When someone believes in me, they believe also in the Father who sent me.

I don't judge the person who hears my words and won't keep them. My mission is to save the world and not to judge it. There is One who will judge in the last days whoever rejects my words.

You have a choice. I am only repeating the words of this One, my Father, whose words lead to now and never-ending life."

No Judgment Zone

Consider - John 12: 44 - 50

Jesus came and lived in the 'no judgment zone.' He says in this passage and in John 3 that he only came to 'save' or rescue, not to condemn or judge.

In the Sermon on the Mount Jesus tells us to not judge others, … or we will be judged in the same way we judge. He also tells us in the Lord's Prayer that we only can ask forgiveness when we forgive others.

Our God is all about showing mercy and withholding judgment. This gives us a clue into his character. His character is all about being gracious, full of compassion, being slow to become angry and being heavy with love. His love is heavy, like a weighted blanket. This is who our God is.

Jesus lived in the 'no judgment zone.'

Jesus does mention that someday down the road there will be a judgment or reckoning day. The judgment on that day will be based on whether we actually heard Jesus' words and did them.

His words connect to his teachings in the passage of the Sheep and the Goats in Matthew 25. Jesus' judgment is based on what they did or did not do for "the least of these brothers and sisters of mine."

John the Writer saw the character of Jesus was not to judge. The character of Jesus was and is to rescue.

Meditate

Jesus shouted to the crowd, "When someone believes in me, they believe also in the Father who sent me.

I don't judge the person who hears my words and won't keep them. My mission is to save the world and not to judge it. There is One who will judge in the last days whoever rejects my words.

You have a choice. I am only repeating the words of this One, my Father, whose words lead to now and never-ending life."

Pray and Go

Be still before God.
Exhale fully and let God fill you.

Meditate

Jesus spent his life loving his followers in the world and would love them to his final act. The Father had placed all things under his feet, so he thought it necessary to scrub the Twelve's feet.

He took off his outer garment, tied a towel around his waist like a servant, poured water in a basin and went around the table scrubbing feet.

Peter put up a fight, but Jesus explained, "Peter, I need to do this or you will have no place on my team. You'll understand later." He even washed Judas' feet knowing he would soon betray him.

Then Jesus shared with the Twelve, "Now I, your Master and Teacher, have scrubbed your feet; it's your turn to scrub each others' feet. Do to others what I have done to you. A servant is not greater than his master. You will be happy if you scrub feet."

Scrubbing feet

Consider - John 13: 1 - 30

John the Writer was the only writer of the four Gospels that recorded this account of Jesus at 'the Last Supper.' It was a story that embodied Jesus' life and character and needed to be passed on to help us in finding John's Jesus.

God washed men's feet!

Throughout Jesus' life he made wine when people ran out, he helped blind people see, he spoke words of life even when he was tired, he healed children, he found 'sinners,' he cast out evil spirits controlling people and he helped paralyzed people walk. His life was lived as a servant to the world. God served us.

Jesus drops and scrubs the dirty feet of his followers. Their master scrubbing his servant's feet. Their God scrubbing their dirty feet. This was another way for us to live. It was a better way. It is God's way.

Jesus flips the organizational hierarchy of the world by his kingdom becoming the new-way leaders serving those under them. This way his servants would do to others as they would want to be done to them.

Love washes feet. Love serves.

This is the God I want to follow.

Washing others feet costs something.

Jesus scrubbed their feet all the way to the Cross.

Meditate

Jesus spent his life loving his followers in the world and would love them to his final act. The Father had placed all things under his feet, so he thought it necessary to scrub the Twelve's feet.

He took off his outer garment, tied a towel around his waist like a servant, poured water in a basin and went around the table scrubbing feet.

Peter put up a fight, but Jesus explained, "Peter, I need to do this or you will have no place on my team. You'll understand later." He even washed Judas' feet knowing he would soon betray him.

Then Jesus shared with the Twelve, "Now I, your Master and Teacher, have scrubbed your feet, it's now your turn to scrub each others' feet. Do to others what I have done to you. A servant is not greater than his master. You will be happy if you scrub feet."

Pray and Go

**Be still before God.
Exhale fully and let God fill you.**

Meditate

Judas left the group at Jesus' command, but the Twelve did not understand he was heading out to betray Jesus.

Jesus said, "It's now time for me to receive glory from the Father, and he will also receive glory through me. I will be leaving you soon… and where I am going you can't follow. So follow my new-Kingdom order, love each other, just like I loved you! This way everyone will know you are my followers. Love each other!"

Peter missed the new-Kingdom order and was distracted by why he could not go where Jesus was going. He then pronounced his commitment to even die for Jesus. Jesus told Peter, "Before the night is over you will deny me three times."

Love

New-Kingdom Order

Consider - John 13: 31 - 38

Peter missed the new-Kingdom order of Jesus. But what is it? His new order is simply to 'love each other.' Imagine a world where that would be true! Imagine God's Kingdom on earth. Imagine a world where selfless love would be the default!

Love each other in the way Jesus loved the Twelve. He mentored them, lived life with them, taught them, provided for them and selflessly died for them.

Love each other in the way I loved you.

It needs to be noted that this command is sandwiched between Judas running off to betray Jesus and Peter being told that he would deny him before the night was over. Jesus had just washed their feet even though this love would not be immediately reciprocated.

Love is something that is given away at no cost to the recipient. Love is something that always costs the one who gives it away. In Scripture we are told "with the measure we measure, it will be measured back to us." So when we love… God gives us more love. It never runs out.

This new-Kingdom order is fully in line with God's command to love God with everything in you, and to love your neighbor as you love yourself.

Love each other. This way the world will know we are followers of the One who loves us.

Meditate

Judas left the group at Jesus' command, but the Twelve did not understand he was heading out to betray Jesus.

Jesus said, "It's now time for me to receive glory from the Father and he will also receive glory through me. I will be leaving you soon… and where I am going you can't follow. So follow my new-Kingdom order, love each other, just like I loved you! This way everyone will know you are my followers. Love each other!"

Pray and Go

Fifty-three

Be still before God.
Exhale fully and let God fill you.

Meditate

Jesus said to the Twelve, "Have no fear even though I am going away. You must trust in God. You must trust in me too.

I'm going to my Father and I will be prepping a room for you. His house is huge.

Have no fear; I will come back here again to get you so you can be with me.

Be still; you know the way... I've told you."

His House is Huge

Consider - John 14: 1 - 4

As John's life unfolded, he heard when each one of the Twelve were martyred for following Jesus. I imagine him recalling these words of Jesus, possibly 50 years later, while imprisoned on an island.

John was still wondering about 'when' Jesus was returning to earth to get the boys. They were now all dead except for John who was still trusting in Jesus.

In this story the Twelve could not comprehend their Messiah was going away. They were afraid. So Jesus paints this beautiful picture of a home, God's home. It was a home where Jesus wanted them to live with him, the Father and the Scared Spirit of God. They would not be orphans but would have a home forever.

Imagine God wanting you with him, forever.

Imagine that he already has a place for you to live in alongside him in God's house, as family.

These words would have been comforting to the Twelve if they actually heard them. All they seemed to hear was Jesus, their master, was going away.

His message to them and to us is…

Have no fear;
trust in God;
trust Jesus;
he's got you!

Meditate

Jesus said to the Twelve, "Have no fear even though I am going away. You must trust in God. You must trust in me too.

I'm going to my Father and I will be prepping a room for you. His house is huge.

Have no fear; I will come back here again to get you so you can be with me.

Be still; you know the way... I've told you."

Pray and Go

Fifty-four

Be still before God.
Exhale fully and let God fill you.

Meditate

Thomas asked Jesus, "You said you are going away, but how can we know where you are going?"

Jesus replied, "I am! I am the way to the Father. I am truth. I am life. No person gets to him without me. Seeing me means you've met the Father."

Philip now spoke, "All we want is to see the Father; please show us."

Jesus replied, "Ah, Philip, don't you know me? Seeing me is seeing the Father. My words are his words. He is living in me and I'm doing his work.

If you have faith in me you will do what I do, and even do greater things since you can ask me and I will directly ask the Father."

I am the Way

Consider - John 14: 5 - 14

Philip and Thomas were still fixated on Jesus' words of him going away. They wondered where and how?

Jesus answered their questions both simply and mysteriously. Simply because the path to God the Father is in Jesus; it is through Jesus.

So the place where Jesus was going was to God his Father, but this was not a destination like Philadelphia or a person they could see. Jesus' answer was simple and also required faith to see.

Having faith to see is a mysterious thing. Jesus earlier explained the Spirit's work like watching the wind. The place of God was invisible and visible in Jesus. The place of God on earth was both now and then.

I hear Jesus saying, "See me; follow me; have no fear; have faith, … you are already with God."

The Twelve genuinely wanted to see God.

Jesus told them. "I am!"

Meditate

Thomas asked Jesus, "You said you are going away, but how can we know where you are going?"

Jesus replied, "I am! I am the way to the Father. I am truth. I am life. No person gets to him without me. Seeing me means you've met the Father."

Philip now spoke, "All we want is to see the Father; please show us."

Jesus replied, "Ah, Philip, don't you know me? Seeing me is seeing the Father. My words are his words. He is living in me and I'm doing his work.

If you have faith in me you will do what I do, and even do greater things since you can ask me and I will directly ask the Father."

Pray and Go

**Be still before God.
Exhale fully and let God fill you.**

Meditate

Jesus continued to speak to the Twelve, "You show
you love me if you obey my order.

If you do, I will ask the Father to send you another
Counselor, like myself, to be with you.
This Counselor is the Spirit that carries truth; he will
be invisible to the world, but so was I.
He will be in you and you will know him.

Soon you only will see me, but the world won't.
At that time you will know I am in the Father,
you are in me, and I am in you!

You show you love me if you obey my orders. I and
the Father will love this one and make our home
with him."

To Obey is to Love

Consider - John 14: 15 - 24

Jesus bookends this short speech to the Twelve (actually eleven now) with the order that to obey him is to love him. We see this in stories of the brotherhood of the Navy Seals and how they will follow their leader to the death because they love him. Love is the greatest motivator, and this kind of real brotherly love begins with obeying. To obey is to love.

The most recent orders of Jesus earlier in this discussion with the Twelve were...
To scrub each others' feet (serve)
and to love each other.

Love is the order most near and dear to the heart of Jesus. Serving others is the means by which we best carry out this love in action. Jesus reminds them to obey.

So if we follow the stream of Jesus' consciousness in this discussion, it appears to be...
Obey my orders to serve each other and love each other and you show me you love me!

Here is a simple test to see where we are in our love for Jesus...
Am I serving others?
Am I loving other?

If so, then I am loving Jesus. If not, then he is full of forgiveness and grace. Repent, believe and follow him in his love.

Meditate

Jesus continued to speak to the Twelve, "You show
you love me if you obey my order.

If you do, I will ask the Father to send you another
Counselor, like myself, to be with you.
This Counselor is the Spirit that carries truth; he will
be invisible to the world, but so was I.
He will be in you and you will know him.

Soon you only will see me, but the world won't.
At that time you will know I am in the Father,
you are in me, and I am in you!

You show you love me if you obey my orders. I and
the Father will love this one and make our home
with him."

Pray and Go

Fifty-six

Be still before God.
Exhale fully and let God fill you.

Meditate

Jesus continued, "This Sacred Spirit of God, your new Counselor, will remind you what I have taught you. He will teach you all things!

This is news of peace to you.
My peace I hand over to you.
This is not the peace from the world you are used to.
It's real.

So although I am going away, have no fear. Don't be troubled! You love me… so be happy I am going to the Father. The one in power over this world is coming to meet me, but have no fear; I have no fear.

The world must see I love the Father and do all he asks. Bring it on."

… from Jesus

Consider - John 14: 25 - 31

Here Jesus teaches the Twelve a few things about peace… because they are worried.

He teaches…

Peace from this world is different from the peace Jesus hands to those who love him. It is not based on the circumstances surrounding one's life, but given directly, supernaturally and internally from Jesus.

Peace is possible through Jesus even when he is not physically here on earth because Jesus sent to his followers the Sacred Spirit, Counselor, or Holy Spirit of God. The word holy means sacred, or someone or something set apart for the use of the divine. The Sacred Spirit is part of what we call, in theology, the Trinity of God; Father, Son and Spirit. The three are one.

Peace is directly from Jesus. His peace is handed over to his Twelve as he approaches his departure from this earth. It is passed from Jesus to his followers. This peace is real and receivable from God.

As you meditate on this passage do not meditate on peace because peace can elude us. Meditate on the Father, on the Son, and in the Spirit, and allow him to hand you real peace.

Meditate

Jesus continued, "This Sacred Spirit of God, your new Counselor, will remind you what I have taught you. He will teach you all things!

This is news of peace to you.
My peace I hand over to you.
This is not the peace from the world you are used to.
It's real.

So although I am going away, have no fear. Don't be troubled! You love me… so be happy I am going to the Father. The one in power over this world is coming to meet me, but have no fear; I have no fear.

The world must see I love the Father and do all he asks. Bring it on."

Pray and Go

Fifty-seven

Be still before God.
Exhale fully and let God fill you.

Meditate

Jesus said, "Let me tell you a story. A gardener cares for the vine in a vineyard.
Every branch that is growing healthy grapes gets pruned after the harvest by the gardener.
Every branch that is not growing healthy grapes is cut off and thrown into the fire. They are already dead. All of this is done to grow more grapes from the vine.

I am the vine. My Father is the gardener. He judges and then cuts. You-branches only grow healthy fruit when they are attached to me.

I am the vine. Hold on to me and my words and I will hold on to you. My words prune your heart.

The Gardener loves me, and I love you, … so hang on to my love."

Hang on to Jesus

Consider - John 15: 1 - 9

This is a very visual story of a vineyard and the work that is done, not to make a great vineyard, but to grow healthy fruit.

Here are two reasons to hang onto Jesus, our vine. Hanging onto Jesus leads to life. Those who love Jesus hang on for 'dear-life' when the winds are blowing and when the storms send heavy rain. Hang on to Jesus so healthy fruits continue to grow out of our lives. This is God's design.

Jesus also says to hang on to him and his love because in him there is a nutritional value to our souls from being loved. His love gives life and allows us to thrive. Jesus is a conduit of the Father's love to us. Hang on to his love. His love is everything we need. John the Writer later repeated these words in 1st John 3 to the early Church. He told them to be a conduit of love... like Jesus.

Here is the connection. Way back in John 3 we are told that God 'so loved the world.' Although I am a recipient of this love, I was never meant to be the ending point for God's love. He loves us and 'the cosmos' so much he sent his Son for us to hang on to so healthy fruit continues to grow in the world. Jesus is bringing restoration to the cosmos. You and I get to be a part of his work.

Hang on to Jesus.

Meditate

Jesus said, "Let me tell you a story. A gardener cares for the vine in a vineyard.
Every branch that is growing healthy grapes gets pruned after the harvest by the gardener.
Every branch that is not growing healthy grapes is cut off and thrown into the fire. They are already dead. All of this is done to grow more grapes from the vine.

I am the vine. My Father is the gardener. He judges and then cuts. You-branches only grow healthy fruit when they are attached to me.

I am the vine. Hold on to me and my words and I will hold on to you. My words prune your heart.

The Gardener loves me, and I love you, … so hang on to my love."

Pray and Go

Fifty-eight

Be still before God.
Exhale fully and let God fill you.

Meditate

Jesus continued to talk about love. "Here's how things need to be done. The laws of God's universe are to
love each other in the way I loved you!

The greatest love in God's universe is for one to lay down his life for his friends!

You are no longer my servants; you are now my friends. The master lets his friends know what he is up to; servants often don't have this privilege.

Friends, I have let you in on all God told me he is up to."

Love

Consider - John 15: 9 - 17

The reason we are taking Jesus' words in small bite-sized chunks is because there is so much goodness we don't want to miss. Are you getting tired of John always talking about love?

Love is the law of God's good universe and the law of the Kingdom of God. In Scripture we are told "God is love." His character is love, so he is full of love. Jesus came here communicating to us God's law and his heart. That was to love.

We recently read of Jesus giving an example of love, and that was to scrub feet. Now he gives us a super-concrete example of the ultimate form of love. Laying down one's life for a friend. Jesus would do this within twenty-four hours of this talk.

This kind of love is the law of God's universe because he says to "Love each other in the way I loved you!"

In America the highest award one could ever receive is the 'Medal of Honor.' This award is given to someone for laying down his or her life for a friend. This is a picture of what Jesus calls 'the greatest love.'

Now Jesus calls his disciples "friends." Imagine God calling you his friend! Shortly he would lay down his life for his friends.

The law of God is love!

Meditate

Jesus continued to talk about love. "Here's how things need to be done; the laws of God's universe are to
love each other in the way I loved you!

The greatest love in God's universe is for one to lay down his life for his friends!

You are no longer my servants; you are now my friends. The master lets his friends know what he is up to; servants often don't have this privilege.

Friends, I have let you in on all God told me he is up to."

Pray and Go

Fifty-nine

Be still before God.
Exhale fully and let God fill you.

Meditate

Jesus said to the Twelve, "Remember what I told
you. No servant is superior to his master.
If I am hated in this place, so will you be.
If I am persecuted here, so will you be.
If people follow my word, they will follow yours too.
This will all happen because of my name.

Who do you belong to? If you belong to the world,
then the world will love you. If you belong to me,
the words I just spoke will be true.

I have chosen you out of the ways of this world.

These people now have no excuse for their sin
because I came and spoke to them. Since they saw
the miracles, they are guilty. They will kick you out
of our house of prayer. Those trying to kill you will
think they are doing God's work."

Belong

Consider - John 15: 18 - 16: 4

Jesus' is preparing the Twelve to consider where they belong. On one side, belonging to the ways or things of this world will allow you to be loved by those in the world. Why? Because you belong with them.

On the flip side, he offers a more difficult choice. If the Twelve belong to Jesus, many will not like them; some will persecute them; they may be excommunicated from their faith community, and some people will even try to kill them.

The systems in place in the world are controlled by, who John refers to, as the prince of this world. He controls governments and religions and the way people think and live.

The prince of this world has power but not ultimate or never-ending power. The death and resurrection of Jesus defeated, and is defeating, this prince. He is heading toward a final destruction.

Belonging. Where do we belong?

Jesus reminds the boys that he chose them to come out of the systems of this world. They belong to him.

Following Jesus promises to be a difficult endeavor at times, but Jesus chose them and he chooses us. We belong to him.

We have a home where we belong.

Meditate

Jesus said to the Twelve, "Remember what I told
you. No servant is superior to his master.
If I am hated in this place, so will you be.
If I am persecuted here, so will you be.
If people follow my word, they will follow yours too.
This will all happen because of my name.

Who do you belong to? If you belong to the world,
then the world will love you. If you belong to me,
the words I just spoke will be true.

I have chosen you out of the ways of this world.

These people now have no excuse for their sin
because I came and spoke to them. Since they saw
the miracles, they are guilty. They will kick you out
of our house of prayer. Those trying to kill you will
think they are doing God's work."

Pray and Go

Sixty

Be still before God.
Exhale fully and let God fill you.

Meditate

"You are distressed because I am leaving you.
Remember, it is good for you, because when I go, I
will send the Counselor.

The Counselor will
be the moral compass for the world,
convict where there is sin,
take my place in showing the world what's right,
and judge the world. The former prince of this
world's reign is now done.

The Counselor will guide you Twelve into even more
truth than I have downloaded to you so far; he'll
download all truth, even what is still ahead.

The Father has made all this mine." Jesus spoke this
to the Twelve.

True North

Consider - John 16: 5 - 15

Compasses can tell us many things. If we set the needle on the compass to 'true north,' we can tell the direction we are heading.

The Sacred or Holy Spirit of God points our world to 'true north.' Up to this point the prince of this world confused our compasses by moving the magnetic pull and pointing our needles to a 'false north.'

Jesus is saying that on the Cross he has defeated this prince. 'True north' is now 'true north' again. Although there is still a strong presence of this prince in our world, Jesus' death and resurrection defeated death and he is making and will make all things good.

Jesus is our 'True North' and the Counselor is our compass showing us what is right and what is sin.

It is fascinating to me that Jesus tells the Twelve that even more truth will be revealed to them… beyond what he told them… by the Counselor. If you think of it and if we believe that all Scripture was originally God-breathed, then the writings of the rest of the New Testament about the Church and things to come may be what Jesus is talking about. The Sacred Spirit of God inspires the authors in writing our Scriptures.

Jesus is our 'True North,' and the Counselor is our guiding compass.

Meditate

"You are distressed because I am leaving you.
Remember, it is good for you, because when I go, I
will send the Counselor.

The Counselor will
be the moral compass for the world,
convict where there is sin,
take my place in showing the world what's right,
and judge the world. The former prince of this
world's reign is now done.

The Counselor will guide you Twelve into even more
truth than I have downloaded to you so far; he'll
download all truth, even what is still ahead.

The Father has made all this mine." Jesus spoke this
to the Twelve.

Pray and Go

Sixty-one

Be still before God.
Exhale fully and let God fill you.

Meditate

The Twelve were still confused while Jesus had his death and soon departure on his mind.

He told this short parable. "It's like this. When a woman is giving birth to a child there is a lot of intense pain, but when her child is born she is overwhelmed with joy.

This is how it will be with you; your distress over my death will be overwhelmed by joy when you see me.

No person ever will ever take that joy away."

Joy!

Consider - John 16: 16 - 24

Considering the intense pain, why would a woman ever choose to give birth to a child? Simply put, the joy of giving life.

Jesus was a master of short stories with punch. This story precedes a new realization of belief in the next section.

Jesus speaks about life, pain and hope. Life has its pain. This pain was brought on us by the fall of Adam and Eve in the Creation account. I, we, perpetuate this pain with our sin. As long as sin is present here, pain will be present. My sin and your sin cause others pain.

Pain in our physical, emotional and spiritual bodies is real and can be intense.
* We were designed to love. Love can cause us pain.
* We were designed with nerve endings to feel. Those nerve endings cause intense pain in our life and Jesus' life.
* We were designed to be with our Creator. Our pulling away from God in our sin can leave us broken, alone, and afraid.

This lesson to the Twelve told them and tells us to hold on, have hope, because joy awaits those following Jesus.

Their pain would soon be real, but Jesus is telling the Twelve hold on; joy is coming... when they see Jesus again.

Meditate

The Twelve were still confused while Jesus had his death and soon departure on his mind.

He told this short parable. "It's like this. When a woman is giving birth to a child there is a lot of intense pain, but when her child is born she is overwhelmed with joy.

This is how it will be with you; your distress over my death will be overwhelmed by joy when you see me.

No person ever will ever take that joy away."

Pray and Go

Sixty-two

Be still before God.
Exhale fully and let God fill you.

Meditate

Jesus said, "Someday I won't need to tell stories for you to understand. I will speak in straight talk and you will get it. At that time you will step forward and ask of the Father anything in my name.

The Father loves you… because you love me and believe he sent me."

Belief happened! The Twelve got it. They saw Jesus in a new light. They said, "We believe that you came from the Father."

Jesus replied, "Finally! Finally you believe. But soon you will run away. In me, embrace peace. I have overcome this old world order."

Belief

Consider - John 16: 25 - 33

The Twelve's faith in Jesus seemed to come in stages, like it does for so many of us.

In the beginning, these twelve guys heard Jesus speak, and when he asked them to come and follow, they did. That requires belief, or something...!? It had been a crazy three-year ride.

Earlier in their journey they came to the belief that Jesus was the Christ/Messiah, or the Anointed One of God. Yet here in John's account, he seems to record a new meaning to who the Twelve thought he was.

It is one thing to believe that Jesus was sent from God in the way an Old Testament prophet was. They were humans who heard from God and followed him in carrying out a specific mission.

It is completely another thing to believe that Jesus arrived here from heaven... like an alien arriving in the clouds. Only this was God's actual Son standing in front of them. He arrived on mission from the place God resided. They now believed this and that Jesus was now returning to that place.

They knew God was Spirit, but now they could see God's face in Jesus. Their hearts were free to see Jesus. They believed more, if that is possible.

Jesus was amazed, "Finally you believe."

This belief carried with it the promise of 'peace.'

Meditate

Jesus said, "Someday I won't need to tell stories for you to understand. I will speak in straight talk and you will get it. At that time you will step forward and ask of the Father anything in my name.

The Father loves you… because you love me and believe he sent me."

Belief happened! The Twelve got it. They saw Jesus in a new light. They said, "We believe that you came from the Father."

Jesus replied, "Finally! Finally you believe. But soon you will run away. In me, embrace peace. I have overcome this old world order."

Pray and Go

Sixty-three

Be still before God.
Exhale fully and let God fill you.

Meditate

Jesus prayed looking up, "My Father, I have completed the work you gave me, so now complete your glory in me. I want to give you the glory you deserve.

You gave me 100% authority to give now and never-ending life to the followers you handed me. This never-ending life they have is… knowing you, the One True God and knowing me, your Son.

Now watch and restore me to the glory I had before this earth began." (Part 1)

Ultimate Team Player

Consider - John 17: 1 - 5

Listening in on Jesus' prayer (Part 1 of 3), John and the Twelve discovered a few things about Jesus.

Jesus' heart was to be a team player. His actions were directed to complete the work given him by his Father. He says that he has now completed all of that work. I have heard it said that his work was the Cross. I would agree, but Jesus says here that his work was completed, and we know that a huge part of Jesus' work was his mentoring of the Twelve. The Twelve would now carry the gospel. Jesus was the Ultimate Team Player.

Jesus' work was to bring honor to the Coach, his Father. He knew who the Coach was and followed his game plan. His work was not easy... we doubted him, we rejected him, we betrayed him and several times tried to kill him. We were not good teammates of Jesus, yet Jesus stayed true to his Coach's game plan to bring honor to him.

Jesus also gives us additional insight into what never-ending life is. It is knowing Jesus and his Father. Earlier in John 3, 5, and 6, we are told to 'believe' to have never-ending life. John 6 records Jesus' words 'feed on me, my flesh and blood,' to have it. John 12 records his words that if we 'lose our life' for Jesus and others we'll have it. Here the 'it,' never-ending life, is not heaven, but 'knowing God.' This knowing is not a knowledge in our heads, but an 'embracing' of him the way one would their spouse. Know Jesus.

Meditate

Jesus prayed looking up, "My Father, I have completed the work you gave me, so now complete your glory in me. I want to give you the glory you deserve.

You gave me 100% authority to give now and never-ending life to the followers you handed me. This never-ending life they have is… knowing you, the One True God and knowing me, your Son.

Now watch and restore me to the glory I had before this earth began." (Part 1)

Pray and Go

Sixty-four

Be still before God.
Exhale fully and let God fill you.

Meditate

Jesus' prayer, "Father, you gave me the Twelve that you always knew. I have shown you to them. They have obeyed me and now believe that I was sent from you. I am asking now for the Twelve only.

Everything is ours, Father. My glory is now completed in them. They will stay here, but I am coming to you. Let your powerful name be their bodyguard. Your name is who you are. Guard them so they become one, just like us.

By my name I was their bodyguard, except for Judas, but we both knew him from the start.

So I ask again for you to be their bodyguard. They are set apart in the world and sent to spread the word of truth. Now I set myself apart for them to also be set apart. (Part 2)

Bodyguard

Consider - John 17: 6 - 19

John the Writer captures the heart of Jesus. He is hours away from his death and prays for the protection of his boys. In this prayer he sets them apart for a sacred use of the Father, to continue the work he had begun.

Jesus did this even though he knew within a few hours they would run away. Our God has a track record of inviting us mess-ups into his work.

Jesus asks the Father to be their bodyguard. The assumption is they need protection. You may remember in an earlier section Jesus tells them that they will be hated, persecuted and even sought out to be killed.

In Jesus' prayer and in his words in the writings of John, I hear Jesus say the name of God is ultimately 'Father.' Father is the name Jesus addressed God in heaven. To Jesus it was a name of endearment, relationship, respect, devotion … it was his Dad. The character of our God is firstly 'Dad.' Great Dads love and great Dads protect. Jesus pleaded with his Father to be bodyguard to these guys.

Then Jesus invites the Twelve into the one-ness of the Trinity of God. God does not need us but made us and invites us into his love, glory and family.

Follow Jesus and you will never be alone.

God was their bodyguard.

Meditate

Jesus' prayer, "Father, you gave me the Twelve that you always knew. I have shown you to them. They have obeyed me and now believe that I was sent from you. I am asking now for the Twelve only.

Everything is ours, Father. My glory is now completed in them. They will stay here, but I am coming to you. Let your powerful name be their bodyguard. Your name is who you are. Guard them so they become one, just like us.

By my name I was their bodyguard, except for Judas, but we both knew him from the start.

So I ask again for you to be their bodyguard. They are set apart in the world and sent to spread the word of truth. Now I set myself apart for them to also be set apart. (Part 2)

Pray and Go

Sixty-five

**Be still before God.
Exhale fully and let God fill you.**

Meditate

Jesus' prayer continues, "Father, I don't only ask this for the Twelve, but also for those who will come after them who will believe in me. I pray that they become one.

I am in you, you are in me, they are in us, and I am in them. One!

I have exchanged their brokenness for the same glory you gave me; their glory is becoming one. This will help the world believe you sent me and love them as you have sent and loved me.

Father, I want them all to be with me. I want them to see my glory and be a part of my glory which existed before this world began.
I am continuing to make you known until the very end… so that the great love you have for me is in them as I am in them." (Part 3)

Be One

Consider - John 17: 20 - 26

It is so amazing to me that when Jesus was confronted by his impending death, he thought to pray for you, for us. He prayed that his followers would step into the one-ness of the Trinity.

God wants to be with us now and for eternity. God wants us to be one, united in him and with him, and united to our sisters and brothers.

My mind goes back to how this all began. God created mankind in his own image, to be like him and to image or mirror him. The story of mankind is about our God making us like him, to image him and then offering to restore us together to him.

This one-ness God desires for us is in Jesus. I love the way Jesus covers all the possibilities of one-ness so there are no questions; "I am in you, you are in me, they are in us, and I am in them. One!"

This idea of being 'in him' is connected to the union of marriage at Creation. Two becoming one. Marriage is a choice, a commitment, and a uniting to another where two become one. The image of marriage is again affirmed by Jesus and then by John in Revelation 19 where the people of God stand before Jesus as a bride prepared to be united to him.

One-ness is very important to Jesus. Be one!

Meditate

Jesus' prayer continues, "Father, I don't only ask this for the Twelve, but also for those who will come after them who will believe in me. I pray that they become one.

I am in you, you are in me, they are in us, and I am in them. One!

I have exchanged their brokenness for the same glory you gave me; their glory is becoming one. This will help the world believe you sent me and love them, as you have sent and loved me.

Father, I want them all to be with me. I want them to see my glory and be a part of my glory which existed before this world began.
I am continuing to make you known until the very end… so that the great love you have for me is in them as I am in them." (Part 3)

Pray and Go

Sixty-six

Be still before God.
Exhale fully and let God fill you.

Meditate

Now this is what love does...
Jesus finished his prayer and went to a usual place
where he would often hang out with the Twelve.
Judas knew it well and led religious armed guards
there to arrest Jesus.

Fully aware of what was going on, Jesus asked
them, "Who do you want?" They responded, "Jesus,
from the town of Nazareth." Jesus answered, "That's
me." The stupefied guards leaned back and fell over.

Jesus pushed the issue and said, "I told you, that's
me. If I am who you want, let the others go." Jesus
stood there like their bodyguard.

Peter jumped forward, grabbed his knife, swung
wildly and randomly cut off a servant's ear. Jesus
told him to put the sword away. I must do this.

Love Fights the Right
Battles

Consider - John 18: 1 - 11

In this account of Jesus, John the Writer reflects on a courageous Jesus who fights for us.

It was now time. The Twelve got it that Jesus was sent from God and was God, so they marched with him toward the fight. Jesus fought the right battles. He was heading to the Cross in an act of love to show the world what love does. This fight was honoring and obedient to his Father.

In that moment John the Writer must have been in shock… partially understanding, but feeling great fear. Many years later, after he reflected on this story, he records a strong and courageous Jesus standing in front of him as a bodyguard. This is what love does.

Malchus, the servant, was in shock as his ear fell to the ground. Peter was acting like Peter did in his impulsiveness. Peter was still learning the ways of Jesus and must have thought, "How can I help?" Jesus tells us in the writings of Matthew that those who draw the sword will also die by the sword.

Jesus fought the right battles, for the Twelve and for the life of the world, in obedience to his Father.

Love fights the right battles.

This is what love does.

Meditate

Now this is what love does…
Jesus finished his prayer and went to a usual place
where he would often hang out with the Twelve.
Judas knew it well and led religious armed guards
there to arrest Jesus.

Fully aware of what was going on Jesus asked them,
"Who do you want?" They responded, "Jesus, from
the town of Nazareth." Jesus answered, "That's me."
The stupefied guards leaned back and fell over.

Jesus pushed the issue and said, "I told you, that's
me. If I am who you want, let the others go." Jesus
stood there like their bodyguard.

Peter jumped forward, grabbed his knife, swung
wildly and randomly cut off a servant's ear. Jesus
told him to put the sword away. I must do this.

Pray and Go

Sixty-seven

Be still before God.
Exhale fully and let God fill you.

Meditate

Jesus was arrested and bound like a criminal. The religious armed guards took him to Annas, a Jewish high priest.

Peter and another of the Twelve followed the procession. The second disciple got them both inside the outdoor courtyard of the high priest.

At the door Peter was asked by a servant girl, "Are you one of Jesus' Twelve?" Peter denied it saying, "No! I am not."

As Jesus was being questioned all night inside, Peter was outside where he denied knowing Jesus two more times. Jesus had predicted Peter's denial and the rooster which now crowed signifying morning had come.

Denial and Grace

Consider - John 18: 12 - 18, 25 - 27

Stay tuned… Peter, the one who first stated that Jesus was actually the Christ, who often put his foot in his mouth, who grabbed his knife, now felt threatened or ashamed and denied knowing Jesus.

It has been said that the Bible is a religious book that often speaks of the failures of its heroes.

Why is this so? The Bible is not a book trying to prove to us what to believe. The writers of the Bible, including John the Writer, are merely recording what they saw or heard. Many of these accounts are very raw and human. The etymology of the word human means 'of the dirt.' We are made from the dirt, and we know that is more often than not how we act. Sometimes the writers give us commentary, but often they just tell the story and let the reader decide. We must all decide what we are going to do with these accounts of Jesus.

In this account Peter failed, but stay tuned; Jesus is not finished with him. Failure and pain are great teachers… and so is grace. The restoration of Peter occurs in chapter 21. Grace is what makes following Jesus different than every other religion.

Peter's denial did not bring on his judgment but opened further the door of the grace of Jesus.

May we examine our hearts to see where we have denied Jesus.

Grace to you.

Meditate

Jesus was arrested and bound like a criminal. The religious armed guards took him to Annas, a Jewish high priest.

Peter and another one of the Twelve followed the procession. The second disciple got them both inside the outdoor courtyard of the high priest.

At the door Peter was asked by a servant girl, "Are you one of Jesus' Twelve?" Peter denied it saying, "No! I am not."

As Jesus was being questioned all night inside, Peter was outside where he denied knowing Jesus two more times. Jesus had predicted Peter's denial and the rooster which now crowed signifying morning had come.

Pray and Go

Sixty-eight

Be still before God.
Exhale fully and let God fill you.

Meditate

As the evening goes on, Annas, the high priest, questions Jesus. Jesus responds, "I did not hide anything. I spoke openly in the synagogues and the temple. Ask the many listeners what I said."

They struck him in the face saying, "You don't speak to the high priest this way."

They took him that night from Annas to Caiaphas, another high priest, then to Pilate, the Roman Governor by morning. The Jews would not enter this Roman building because under their rules it would make them unclean for their Passover meal.

Pilate asked what the charges were against Jesus. He responded, "Charge him yourselves."

The religious leaders answered, "We want to execute him, but we are not allowed."

Hypocrisy

Consider - John 18: 19 - 24, 28 - 32

The built-up hatred inside these religious leaders toward Jesus moved them to plot an innocent man's arrest in secrecy, prosecute him without due process, desire to kill him out of envy and blindness, crave blood shed … and they still wished to have their hands clean for that day's Jewish Passover meal celebrating freedom with their families. Hypocrisy loomed large.

Their Passover celebration was far greater to them than America's Independence Day. They remembered over one million of their ancestors who were living in the slavery of Egyptian oppression becoming free.

The penultimate symbol of their freedom celebration was a slaughtered lamb. On that day, the blood of innocent lambs was placed on their ancestor's doorposts so the Angel of Death would 'pass over' their home and free their people. The lamb was eaten that evening, preparing the people for a long journey out of Egypt at daybreak.

The irony here is that at daybreak an innocent Jesus stood before these leaders condemned. He was the innocent slaughtered lamb given for the freedom from sin and death for the life the world. They missed it. On this day these men would go home to their families to celebrate another freedom.

Hypocrisy stands dirty and condemned in the face of this innocent man.

Hatred and envy brings blindness to us all. May we look into the face of Jesus to see.

Meditate

As the evening goes on, Annas, the high priest, questions Jesus. Jesus responds, "I did not hide anything. I spoke openly in the synagogues and the temple. Ask the many listeners what I said."

They struck him in the face saying, "You don't speak to the high priest this way."

They took him that night from Annas to Caiaphas, another high priest, then to Pilate, the Roman Governor by morning. The Jews would not enter this Roman building because under their rules it would make them unclean for their Passover meal.

Pilate asked what the charges were against Jesus. He responded, "Charge him yourselves."

The religious leaders answered, "We want to execute him, but we are not allowed."

Pray and Go

Sixty-nine

Be still before God.
Exhale fully and let God fill you.

Meditate

Pilate asked Jesus, "Are you actually the Jewish king?" Jesus responded, "Did someone tell you that, or did you think of that yourself?"

"Am I Jewish? No! Your own people gave you up. What ticked them off?" Pilate

"My kingdom is another world. If it was here, my servants would defend me." Jesus

"So you are a king!" Pilate

"Yes, this is why I was born. This is why I moved into your world… to show what's true. Those on truth's side hear me." Jesus

Pilate replied, "Ha! What is truth?" Then he stood before the Jewish crowd now forming and said, "This guy has done nothing wrong. Shall I release him for your Passover?" The crowd yelled, "No."

King!?

Consider - John 18: 33 - 40

Embedded in this account is the idea of truth. The Romans were noted in history as being very philosophical. Later in the book of Acts the Twelve would stand in philosophical debate with Roman citizens.

In most discussions of philosophy, truth is relative. In Pilate's mind, truth was debatable.

The ongoing debate was whether Jesus was a king. The Jewish leaders said he claimed to be. To Pilate there was no king but Caesar. Pilate wanted to know.

Jesus affirmed he was a king from another world. The word world in Scripture often refers to the systems and order of this place. The world is the way this place operates when we don't follow the kingship of our God over all Creation.

God made mankind and told us to rule this world well in the way our good God would rule. This ruling well carries with it the stewardship of caring for animals, the garden, institutions and of course others. Jesus showed us that ruling well is selflessly serving others.

Jesus brought God's Kingdom back in full force to the world.

Jesus is King.

Meditate

Pilate asked Jesus, "Are you actually the Jewish king?" Jesus responded, "Did someone tell you that, or did you think of that yourself?"

"Am I Jewish? No! Your own people gave you up. What ticked them off?" Pilate

"My kingdom is another world. If it was here my servants would defend me." Jesus

"So you are a king!" Pilate

"Yes, this is why I was born. This is why I moved into your world… to show what's true. Those on truth's side hear me." Jesus

Pilate replied, "Ha! What is truth?" Then he stood before the Jewish crowd now forming and said, "This guy has done nothing wrong. Shall I release him for your Passover?" The crowd yelled, "No."

Pray and Go

Seventy

Be still before God.
Exhale fully and let God fill you.

Meditate

Pilate had Jesus bound and the solders whipped him mercilessly. Strike after strike on his back.

Because of Jesus' claim to be king, the Roman soldiers made him a crown of twisted thorns and forced it on his head.

Next they put a purple robe on him. They took turns going up to him saying, "Praise the king of the Jews!" and punching him in the face.

Bound and Beaten

Consider - John 19: 1 - 3

The Romans were brutal in their punishment and here in their mockery. The book of Isaiah tells us Jesus was wounded and bruised for our sin. Pause and take that in.

The Jewish leaders accused him based on their law, and the Roman law carried out the sentence. This was because the Jewish leaders were under Roman rule. They did not like the rule but used it to beat and kill Jesus.

History tells us that the Romans were strong in the practice of their law and ruthless in punishment. Jesus could have come at any time in history. Why did God pick such a time? Pause and take this in.

Jesus was most likely flogged or whipped under what is believed the Roman law of the time. One could be beaten up to forty strikes, and the whip often contained objects that would cut, tear and rip skin.

We know from our own lives that when something 'costs us something' it often means more to us. In this case we mean a lot to Jesus. Our salvation cost our Brother and Rescuer much. Could knowing all that Jesus went through for us help us love him more?

Our brother's face was punched by a cowardly mob of solders over and over again. He took it all because he loved us much.

Thank you Jesus

Meditate

Pilate had Jesus bound and the solders whipped him mercilessly. Strike after strike on his back.

Because of Jesus' claim to be king, the Roman soldiers made him a crown of twisted thorns and forced it on his head.

Next they put a purple robe on him. They took turns going up to him saying, "Praise the king of the Jews!" and punching him in the face.

Pray and Go

**Be still before God.
Exhale fully and let God fill you.**

Meditate

Pilate marched a beaten Jesus in a purple robe
before the ravenous crowd saying, "I find no laws
this man has broken. Here he is."
The Jewish priests screamed, "Crucify him! Kill him!"

Pilate said, "You take him; he is innocent." Then the
priests said, "Under our law anyone claiming to be
the Son of God must die."

Pilate was terrified and asked Jesus, "Where are you
really from?" Jesus stood in silence. Pilate
demanded, "Speak to me. I have the power to
crucify or free you!"

Jesus replied, "Your only power is what God gave
you. The one who sold me out is far more guilty."

Pilate was trapped between the truth and the
people and said, "Here is your King!" The leaders
broke their own law responding, "Caesar is our only
king." Pilate caved and sent Jesus to be crucified.

Silence

Consider - John 19: 4 - 16

The world is screaming at Jesus and he remained silent. The priests were screaming for his murder. The solders were hungry for blood. The mob was revolting... and Jesus stood in silence.

In Pilate's inner turmoil he wanted to free Jesus. He had broken no laws. He had Jesus beaten in hopes the thirst for blood of the Jewish priests would be satisfied.

Once Pilate heard the claim 'Jesus was God's Son' he was terrified. The Roman connection with mythology allowed this to be a possibility. Kings were strong, but gods were stronger.

He tried to free Jesus.

Jesus stood in silence.

Jesus made no effort to free himself.

Jesus' time had come. He must die for the life of the world.

John the Writer was amazed by Jesus.

The world was screaming at Jesus and he stood in silence.

Jesus entrusted himself to his Father, "the One who judges justly."

Meditate

Pilate marched a beaten Jesus in a purple robe out before the ravenous crowd saying, "I find no laws this man has broken. Here he is."
The Jewish priests screamed, "Crucify him! Kill him!"

Pilate said, "You take him, he is innocent." Then the priests said, "Under our law anyone claiming to be the Son of God must die."

Pilate was terrified and asked Jesus, "Where are you really from?" Jesus stood in silence. Pilate demanded, "Speak to me. I have the power to crucify or free you!"

Jesus replied, "Your only power is what God gave you. The one who sold me out is far more guilty."

Pilate was trapped between the truth and the people and said, "Here is your King!" The leaders broke their own law responding, "Caesar is our only king." Pilate caved and sent Jesus to be crucified.

Pray and Go

Seventy-two

**Be still before God.
Exhale fully and let God fill you.**

Meditate

The solders took Jesus and forced him to carry the wooden cross he would hang on. The crowd went with them through the streets and up a hill called "The Place of the Skull."

Here they lifted Jesus up on his cross between two criminals. Although the priests objected… Pilate had a sign placed on Jesus' cross. The sign read in Aramaic, Latin and Greek, "Jesus from Nazareth, The King of the Jews."

The soldiers each took Jesus' clothes, leaving him naked on the cross.

His mother Mary, Mary Magdalene, and two others stood and watched him die. "The one of the Twelve whom Jesus loved" was also there. Jesus, still caring for others, asked him to take in and care for his mother. After the crucifixion he did.

Horrific

Consider - John 19: 16 - 27

Imagine a place being so horrific it is called "The Place of the Skull." We know this place was Golgotha, and some say this hill looked like a skull. This was the place they murdered Jesus.

Imagine, after being subjected to much torture and being up all night without food and proper hydration, someone making you carry the cross beams of your own torture device through town in front of a crowd and up a hill where eventually you would be hammered to wood naked and lifted up to die in front of a crowd. Imagine the horror.

Jesus carried his cross. Jesus carried our cross.

This account of Jesus' death shows just how horrific our sins actually are. We can't see how horrific our envy, pride, wants, hate, judgment, selfishness,... are to God and on ourselves and this world. We only need to read the news to see the effects of our sin on this world.

God so much loved the world he gave...
he gave his only Son in payment for our sin...
so that anyone who looks to him and believes would have now and never-ending life...
with him.

It has been said in many ways ... "Our sin is great, but God's love is greater."

May we live today in gratitude to our God.

Meditate

The solders took Jesus and forced him to carry the wooden cross he would hang on. The crowd went with them through the streets and up a hill called "The Place of the Skull."

Here they lifted Jesus up on his cross in between two criminals. Although the priests objected... Pilate had a sign placed on Jesus' cross. The sign read in Aramaic, Latin and Greek, "Jesus from Nazareth, The King of the Jews."

The soldiers each took Jesus' clothes leaving him naked on the cross.

His mother Mary, Mary Magdalene, and two others stood and watched him die. "The one of the Twelve whom Jesus loved" was also there. Jesus still caring for others asked him to take in and care for his mother. After the crucifixion he did.

Pray and Go

Be still before God.
Exhale fully and let God fill you.

Meditate

About 3:00 in the afternoon Jesus said, "I'm thirsty."
A sponge of wine-vinegar was lifted up to him.
Then he said, "It's finished!"

All of his work was completed, so he bowed his head
as if to pray and freed his spirit up to the Father...
Jesus died.

It was Friday, the day before the Jewish Sabbath.
Being the Preparation Day, the religious leaders
wanted Jesus dead quickly so they could be finished
their work to prepare for their Sabbath-rest.

They asked for Jesus' legs to be broken so he would
die quicker. He was already dead when they got
there. They pierced his side to confirm his death.
Blood and water flowed out of him. This fulfilled a
prediction of Zechariah in chapter twelve of his
book.

It's Finished!

Consider - John 19: 28 - 37

John mentions that all of Jesus' work on earth was now completed. With a 'check mark' and 'exclamation' John said it was so.

Showing he was God and all things were under his control including life, he released his own spirit to the Father for his care. Jesus had said earlier in his life, "No one can take my life, ... I give it up for the life of the world." Jesus gave up his life freely for us.

With a final request of a drink Jesus confirmed his humanity. Jesus was thirsty. Jesus had a physical body in the same way we do. Then proving his power over life, he gave his up and freed himself from this broken world.

Death, to a follower of Jesus, is freedom and a celebration to the never-ending life and power of God.

"I'm thirsty." "It's finished!"

"I give my life for the life of the world." (Check!)

Now what... for his followers? Was this victory or defeat?

"It's finished!"

Meditate

About 3:00 in the afternoon Jesus said, "I'm thirsty."
A sponge of wine-vinegar was lifted up to him.
Then he said, "It's finished!"

All of his work was completed, so he bowed his head
as if to pray and freed his spirit up to the Father...

Jesus died.

Pray and Go

Be still before God.
Exhale fully and let God fill you.

Meditate

Jesus was dead.

Now a secret follower of Jesus enters the story. His name was Joseph from the town of Arimathea. He had followed Jesus in secret because he was afraid of the religious Jews.

Joseph got the okay from Pilate to take Jesus' body for burial. Nick, the one who was also afraid and came earlier to Jesus at nighttime with questions, accompanied Joseph. Nick brought the spices and they wrapped his body.

Then they laid Jesus' body in a tomb nearby. The tomb had never been used. They closed the opening with a large stone.

They put Jesus' body to rest.

Jesus Inspires Courage

Consider - John 19: 38 - 42

The courage of Jesus in the past few entries has been evident as he marched toward his own cross. This is in direct contrast to the two men who came for Jesus' body.

Joseph, not Jesus' earthly Dad, was afraid to follow Jesus out in the open because he feared the religious leaders kicking him out of the temple. This was their religious community and also their social community.

Nick, who early on snuck in to ask Jesus questions at night, was actually one of the Pharisees, a religious leader. He, like Joseph, would not follow Jesus openly at that time because of the wrath of fellow religious leaders.

Somehow over time while observing Jesus they must have come to know each other and discussed Jesus. Now they took a huge risk of asking the local Roman leader, who just killed their Master, for his body.

Would they be unclean for the Sabbath? Would they be kicked out of the community?

John the Writer records this account of how the courageous Jesus inspired these two men.

May knowing Jesus inspire our courage today.

Meditate

Jesus was dead.

Now a secret follower of Jesus enters the story. His name was Joseph from the town of Arimathea. He had followed Jesus in secret because he was afraid of the religious Jews.

Joseph got the okay from Pilate to take Jesus' body for burial. Nick, the one who was also afraid and came earlier to Jesus at nighttime with questions, accompanied Joseph. Nick brought the spices and they wrapped his body.

Then they laid Jesus' body in a tomb nearby. The tomb had never been used. They closed the opening with a large stone.

They put Jesus' body to rest.

Pray and Go

Seventy-five

Be still before God.
Exhale fully and let God fill you.

Meditate

It was now before dawn on Sunday morning and Mary Magdalene went to the tomb. In the darkness she found the stone covering; it was rolled away.

Immediately she ran to tell Peter and the one Jesus loved crying, "They have taken the Lord. We don't know where."

We both raced to the tomb. I, John, got there first; but when Peter got there, he ran straight inside. Only the burial wrap remained.

Then I stepped in the tomb. I believed, but I still could not fully understand it all.

What just happened?

Consider - John 20: 1 - 9

Imagine if it was so. Someone you loved who had died vanished from the place they were buried. This left his followers wondering what just happened.

Jesus had talked about going away. He even said he was going to the Father. Today we would believe this of a saint dying and their soul going to be with God. In this case Jesus had something different in mind. He had to beat death... so we could also beat death.

It appears that Jesus was unwrapped... and gone! What just happened?

Mary from Magdalene came super early in the morning. It appears she was not alone because when she told the men, she said "we." The other Gospels also support this. Then she ran.

Peter and John (called the one Jesus loved) heard; then they ran. There is even some competitive rivalry here in who ran faster to the tomb, although John gives Peter credit for entering the tomb first.

This Mary, Peter and John were some of the most profound leaders recorded in church history, possibly because of their profound love and commitment to the Lord.

Jesus was gone... death could not hold him. John believed but did not understand. Who would have?

Imagine if it was true.

Meditate

It was now before dawn on Sunday morning and Mary Magdalene went to the tomb. In the darkness she found the stone covering; it was rolled away.

Immediately she ran to tell Peter and the one Jesus loved crying, "They have taken the Lord. We don't know where."

We both raced to the tomb. I, John, got there first, but when Peter got there he ran straight inside. Only the burial wrap remained.

Then I stepped in the tomb, I believed, but I still could not fully understanding it all.

Pray and Go

Be still before God.
Exhale fully and let God fill you.

Meditate

The men left and Mary remained there at the tomb weeping. Then she looked in again and saw two angels in brilliant white seated at the head and foot of where Jesus had been lying.

They spoke to her, "Why are you weeping?" Mary said, "People have taken my Lord and I don't know where."

Jesus emerged behind her asking, "Excuse me ma'am, why are you weeping,… who are you looking for?" Mary, confused, thinking Jesus was a caretaker, said, "If you have moved him please tell me."

To get her attention Jesus said boldly, "Mary!" Mary went to grab hold of him, "Teacher!" Jesus replied, "Not yet! I have not completed my journey to the Father and back again. I came to comfort you. Go tell my brothers you saw me."

For Others

Consider - John 20: 10 - 18

Jesus cared for Mary. Jesus also cares deeply for you.

Jesus had finished his very hard work here and probably wished to run away. To live here or there with the Father is not a tough choice.

Jesus paused his journey to meet Mary in her confusion and grief. Jesus cared for Mary. Jesus has always been for others, for us.

Jesus seems to show up today in people's lives when they seek him or need him the most. Why? He's always there, he's always here with us, but we don't see him. We see a caretaker when he is right there as caregiver. When we need him the most, he grabs our attention by saying our name, "Scott!"

John Mark, the writer of the book of Mark, in his account of Jesus in chapter 16 tells us that this Mary had seven demons cast out of her by Jesus. Imagine the freedom, the transformation, and the rescue she had experienced. This may help explain the ravenous passion with which she pursued Jesus.

Jesus rescued Mary from Magdalene. Jesus offers us that same rescue. Jesus cares for us.

May we grab hold of Jesus today.

Meditate

The men left and Mary remained there at the tomb weeping. Then she looked in again and saw two angels in brilliant white seated at the head and foot of where Jesus had been lying.

They spoke to her, "Why are you weeping?" Mary said, "People have taken my Lord and I don't know where."

Jesus emerged behind her asking, "Excuse me ma'am, why are you weeping,… who are you looking for?" Mary, confused, thinking Jesus was a caretaker, said, "If you have moved him please tell me."

To get her attention Jesus said boldly, "Mary!" Mary went to grab hold of him, "Teacher!" Jesus replied, "Not yet! I have not completed my journey to the Father and back again. I came to comfort you. Go tell my brothers you saw me."

Pray and Go

Seventy-seven

Be still before God.
Exhale fully and let God fill you.

Meditate

That same day... Sunday evening, the Twelve were all together locked in a room. They were afraid of what the priests might do to them. Jesus entered through the walls.

He greeted them in their fears, "Have my peace in you!"

He called them over and showed them the holes in his hands and side. Joy flooded their souls.

"Have my peace in you! I'm now sending you out in the same way the Father sent me to do his work." Jesus exhaled on them and asked them to inhale the Sacred Spirit of God.

"By the Spirit grant forgiveness to anyone. If they receive it, it is as if they already were forgiven since the beginning of time."

Flood of Joy

Consider - John 20: 19 - 23

Fear robs us of joy. Jesus meets these men in their fear and offers them a greeting. This was not just any greeting but a greeting of his peace.

When we look to Jesus instead of the problems the next day will bring, when we grab onto Jesus instead of the hurt others have thrown our way, when we receive Jesus' peace instead of dwelling on one who sees us as an enemy, we can experience peace. Real peace is deep inside us. Real peace is from Jesus.

"Have my peace in you!"

The peace Jesus offered these men became a flood of joy. Fear holds us down… fear holds us under… the way Jonah felt in the belly of a large fish in the depths of the sea.

Jesus' peace floods our souls. This flood washes us clean, gives us new breath, and enables us to experience joy.

Joy is beyond temporary. Joy can be close in times of struggle. The Twelve would now need this peace. They would be setting out on a new journey without Jesus being physically with them, doing his work.

Jesus exhaled the Spirit of God on them, in the same way in John 1, John described Jesus as "The Long Exhale" of the Father. They had the Sacred Spirit of God in them now so they would never be alone.

You are never alone. Have Jesus' peace in you.

Meditate

That same day... Sunday evening the Twelve were all together locked in a room. They were afraid of what the priests might do to them. Jesus entered through the walls.

He greeted them in their fears, "Have my peace in you!"

He called them over and showed them the holes in his hands and side. Joy flooded their souls.

"Have my peace in you! I'm now sending you out in the same way the Father sent me to do his work." Jesus exhaled on them and asked them to inhale the Sacred Spirit of God.

"By the Spirit grant forgiveness to anyone. If they receive it, it is as if they already were forgiven since the beginning of time."

Pray and Go

Seventy-eight

Be still before God.
Exhale fully and let God fill you.

Meditate

"Thomas, we saw the Lord!" declared the Twelve.

Thomas replied, "That's crazy! I will only believe it if I can stick my fingers in the holes in his hands and side."

The following week the Twelve were still locking themselves in the same room. Jesus came back and said, "Have my peace in you! Thomas, put your fingers in my hands and side. Turn your non-believing into believing!"

Thomas believed, "My Lord, my God!"

Jesus, "Your sight has brought you faith; how eternally happy will those be who won't see me and still believe."

No-See Faith

Consider - John 20: 24 - 29

Jesus is talking about us. That is so cool that he had us on his mind. He truly came for the life of the world. He is talking about us who choose to follow him without ever actually seeing him. This is a 'no-see faith.'

In this story Thomas is still struggling with believing in something that can't, or doesn't, happen. Let's not be too hard on Thomas because people just don't come back to life. He just witnessed his brutal murder.

He wanted to see, touch Jesus.

During his time on earth there were many who saw and heard Jesus and still did not believe. Today there are many of us who have never seen Jesus and believe. We believe in the impossible. We believe in the ridiculous. We believe in a dead man who came back to life… and this man was God.

Somehow Jesus gives us eyes to see. Somehow he gives us 'a knowing' that is more real than seeing or touching. Jesus empowers us to have a 'no-see faith.'

Thank you, Jesus, for the salvation you offer us sinful people. Thank you, Jesus, that you rescue anyone who calls on your name. Help us believe even when we cannot see you.

We believe… Our Lord, our God.

Meditate

"Thomas, we saw the Lord!" declared the Twelve.

Thomas replied, "That's crazy! I will only believe it if I can stick my fingers in the holes in his hands and side."

The following week the Twelve were still locking themselves in the same room. Jesus came back and said, "Have my peace in you! Thomas, put your fingers in my hands and side. Turn your non-believing into believing!"

Thomas believed, "My Lord, my God!"

Jesus, "Your sight has brought you faith; how eternally happy will those be who won't see me and still believe."

Pray and Go

Seventy-nine

Be still before God.
Exhale fully and let God fill you.

Meditate

One book could never contain all of the God-Only Things that Jesus did. He did these miracles right in front of us.

I, John, recorded these things to help you believe that Jesus is the Christ, the promised Messiah, and the Son of God...

So that in your faith in Jesus you would have real life.

Life

Consider - John 20: 30 - 31

Consider life. John the Writer wrote this book so that we would have faith in Jesus to find life, real life.

This word life is and has been translated in so many different ways. Life, in our English language at its most raw and basic premise, is 'to exist.' Plants do it, animals do it and humans do it for a little while.

To have life is 'to exist.' One of the definitions of 'exist,' is to live… or to thrive in an adverse place. This world can often be an adverse place.

Way back in the original story of Creation and in the fall of man is a tree. This tree symbolizes something made by God that was good in Creation. Yet there were two trees; the Tree of Life and the Tree That Opened Our Eyes to Good and Evil. Mankind ate of the second tree and we still do. Our eyes are now open to evil, and we are great at practicing sin.

Our sin wrecked our relationship with our Good-God and hurts the entire cosmos. Mankind would no longer live forever. Death weighs heavy on us all.

Jesus hung on a Tree. His death offers us life, real life. In Christianity, so much emphasis has been placed on our living forever that we fail to see Jesus' offer is to be alive now, to have Life, and to exist well now. The life Jesus offers is both now and never-ending. Eat of this first tree. Eat of the Tree of Life.

Meditate

One book could never contain all of the God-Only-Things that Jesus did. He did these miracles right in front of us.

I, John, recorded these things to help you believe that Jesus is the Christ, the promised Messiah, and the Son of God…

So that in your faith in Jesus you would have real life.

Pray and Go

Eighty

Be still before God.
Exhale fully and let God fill you.

Meditate

Five of the Twelve decided to go out at night to the
Sea of Galilee to fish.

Very early the next morning, resurrected Jesus
yelled out to them from the shore, "Friends, did you
catch any?" They did not know it was Jesus. They
yelled back, "No."

The voice from the shore said to throw their fishing
net over to the other side of the boat and they
would catch some. Listening, they did it and caught
so many they could not pull them into the boat.

John immediately realized it was the Lord and told
Peter. Peter jumped in and swam to shore. They had
been about a football field away from shore.

Vocation

Consider - John 21: 1 - 8

What was the work now of the Twelve? Early in their journey with Jesus he pulled many of these fishermen away from their profession with these words, "Come, follow me." In the book of Mark we are told that Jesus then said to them, "… and I will make you into fishers of men."

These guys had now followed Jesus for three years. In that time they learned to be fishers of men; they saw how Jesus gathered those the Father had given to him.

Now the resurrected Jesus was back but not always with them, and they reverted back to their original profession, fishing.

Jesus was a fantastic teacher using imagery, and here he found them possibly reconsidering their old profession, or at least wanting to provide for themselves. He began calling them back to gathering humans to the Father.

As this story of Jesus is unpacked, we sense that Jesus is reminding these leaders to not just return to their profession but to find their vocation.

One's vocation is a deep sense of their calling to the work they were made to do in this broken world. A profession is all about picking a career. A vocation is listening to our Maker and Caller and paying attention to what he is doing around you. A vocation is not concerned with money or importance but in passionately following Jesus.

May we pay attention to Jesus.

Meditate

Five of the Twelve decided to go out at night to the Sea of Galilee to fish.

Very early the next morning, resurrected Jesus yelled out to them from the shore, "Friends, did you catch any?" They did not know it was Jesus. They yelled back, "No."

The voice from the shore said to throw their fishing net over to the other side of the boat and they would catch some. Listening, they did it and caught so many they could not pull them into the boat.

John immediately realized it was the Lord and told Peter. Peter jumped in and swam to shore. They had been about a football field away from shore.

Pray and Go

Eighty-one

Be still before God.
Exhale fully and let God fill you.

Meditate

When the Twelve's boat came to shore, they noticed that Jesus had a fire roaring and ready to grill some fish. He also had some bread.

Jesus asked them to bring over some fish. Peter went and helped drag the net ashore. Then Jesus said, "Come, let's have breakfast."

Jesus took the bread and fish and passed them out, reminding them of how he had fed the thousands.

This was the third time Jesus appeared to the Twelve after his resurrection.

Breaking Bread

Consider - John 21: 9 - 14

John the Writer records this very special time with their Lord. The resurrected Jesus came to them when they could not supply for themselves.

The hospitable Jesus prepared a fire, gave them bread and grilled their fish. Jesus cared that people had food to eat. He hospitably invited these men to a place that felt like home, and he cared for them.

Jesus broke bread. In this account of Jesus we often fixate on the fish. Yet here we see, tucked into the story, Jesus having and sharing bread. We see Jesus breaking it and passing it out to the five men in the same way he had done at the Last Supper and when he fed the 5,000.

In those two stories, the Twelve learned that when we break bread with Jesus, there is always enough. Jesus is and gives everything we need.

By now the Twelve were also seeing the connection between the broken bread and Jesus' broken body given for them. Maybe this is why Jesus' followers thank God before they break bread and eat. We know by the reminder of breaking bread that Jesus gave his body so we would have all we need.

This symbol was significant to the early church. In the book of 'the Acts of the Twelve' we are told that the early church all came together to break bread. Breaking bread together reminded them of Jesus… the hospitality of giving his body for them.

In breaking bread Jesus invites us home.

Meditate

When the Twelve's boat came to shore they noticed that Jesus had a fire roaring and ready to grill some fish. He also had some bread.

Jesus asked them to bring over some fish. Peter went and helped drag the net ashore. Then Jesus said, "Come, let's have breakfast."

Jesus took the bread and fish and passed them out, reminding them of how he had fed thousands.

This was the third time Jesus appeared to the Twelve after his resurrection.

Pray and Go

Eighty-two

Be still before God.
Exhale fully and let God fill you.

Meditate

After breakfast Jesus looked at Peter and said, "Simon, do you love me even more than you love these?" Peter replied, "Yes, I do, Master; you know I do." Jesus responded, "Feed my young sheep."

Then Jesus asked Peter again, "Do you love me?" Peter's response was the same, and Jesus replied, "Care for my sheep."

Jesus asked Peter a third time, "Do you love me?" Peter, now feeling hurt, replied, "Master, I know nothing, and you know everything; you know I love you!?" Jesus replied, "Spend your life feeding my sheep… you must follow me."

I, John, give witness that these stories of Jesus… what he said and did is true.

Full Circle Restoration

Consider - John 21: 15 - 25

John's accounts of Jesus and the Twelve have now gone full circle. Jesus changes lives, and Peter may be one of the most vivid examples ever recorded.

John begins the story of Jesus calling the Twelve to come and follow him. In this final story he is still calling Peter and the Twelve to follow him. But the first thing he needed to do was restore Peter.

God loves to change the lives of us sinners for his glory.

You will remember that the leader Peter denied knowing Jesus three times on the night leading up to Jesus' crucifixion. Imagine saying you would die for your Master and within twelve hours denying you know him.

Peter must have felt like a fraud; he must have felt he was disqualified for service; he must have felt he was "not good enough." In this story, Jesus shows us what grace is like in restoring Peter to take over his work once he left this earth. With three affirmations of love… "Do you love me?" and then passionate pleas to follow him in the restoring work of caring for his sheep, Jesus reinstated Peter as a leader in his work.

Jesus, we, too, love you. You love us and have restored us, with Peter, to be a part of your restoring work and message in this world. You came for the life of the world and we, too, wish to live that way. In our sin, we, like Peter, are never good enough on our own, but that does not matter… for what matters is that we are deeply LOVED by you.

Meditate

After breakfast Jesus looked at Peter and said, "Simon, do you love me even more than you love these?" Peter replied, "Yes, I do, Master; you know I do." Jesus responded, "Feed my young sheep."

Then Jesus asked Peter again, "Do you love me?" Peter's response was the same, and Jesus replied, "Care for my sheep."

Jesus asked Peter a third time, "Do you love me?" Peter now feeling hurt replied, "Master I know nothing, and you know everything; you know I love you!?" Jesus replied, "Spend your life feeding my sheep… you must follow me."

I, John, give witness that these stories of Jesus… what he said and did is true.

Pray and Go

(And now for John's opening summary of Jesus)
Eighty-three

Be still before God.
Exhale fully and let God fill you.

Meditate

Jesus is The Long Exhale of the Father.
Now breathe him in.

Jesus is The Expression of the Father.
Listen to him.

The Long Exhale existed from the very beginning of
time. He was present with God and was, in fact,
God.
Life was and is in him.

Everything that exists was made through The Long
Exhale of the Father.
Jesus is The Full Expression of who the Father is.

The Long Exhale

Consider - John 1: 1 - 3

After taking in all of the stories of Jesus, John describes him as the Word of God, or The Long Exhale of God. The Long Exhale brought about Creation; the earth and planets, the animals and humans, the seasons and gravity, love and life. Jesus is the breath of God that brought our existence. John witnessed this first hand in Jesus' miracles.

The Long Exhale is God's Expression of himself to us.

When we experience great emotion like pain, frustration or joy, we often express ourselves with breath. It's as if we can't keep it in. It is said that we "swear under our breath," or we sigh when experiencing deep pain. When we experience great joy, it is as if our breath cannot remain in us and comes up easily in relief. In great emotion we exhale… and then our words follow.

We cannot have words without an exhale.

John the Writer had the privilege of spending three years with Jesus. The Long Exhale and Expression of the Father stood and spoke, sat and ate, cried and loved, walked and breathed the same air.

Imagine sitting with and looking into the face of God. As John listened to Jesus, he felt life return to his soul. Peter said, "Who else should we follow? You have the words of Life, eternal life. We believe and know deep down that you are the Holy One promised by God."

Meditate

Jesus is The Long Exhale of the Father.
Now breathe him in.

Jesus is The Expression of the Father.
Listen to him.

The Long Exhale existed from the very beginning of time. He was present with God and was in fact God. Life was and is in him.

Everything that exists was made through The Long Exhale of the Father.
Jesus is The Full Expression of who the Father is.

Pray and Go

Eighty-four

Be still before God.
Exhale fully and let God fill you.

Meditate

From the origin of our time God spoke everything
into existence out of darkness.
Genesis 1

From the origin of our time God exhaled Jesus,
speaking everything into existence out of darkness.

The Long Exhale began all life... and he today still
ignites life in mankind.

This present darkness cannot overcome that light.
John 1

Creator - Life Giver

Consider - John 1: 1 - 5

As John reflected on the work of Jesus his mind went back to Creation. He witnessed first-hand the re-creating of life in him and others in the same way God brought life to this world in Jesus.

Jesus was there at the beginning, and Jesus was God before this world began. All things were made by him and through him. He is the Creator of life. While here, Jesus proved this by breathing life back into people who had died, re-creating life in the sick, freeing the possessed from bondage and even controlling the wind. Jesus has 100% authority over all creation.

Breathe. It is interesting to me that you don't have to teach a newborn to breathe. Jesus, from Creation, continues to ignite that spark of life in us. We often don't even think about our breath unless we have asthma or are under stress.

Spiritual breath. Often we forget to breathe in Jesus. It is so easy to walk around in this world breathing in the toxic air that harms us. We fail to pursue Jesus for our oxygen. He is still our Life Giver, physically and spiritually. Exhale fully the toxic air of this world, and breathe in deeply the light of Jesus.

Jesus is our Maker and Life Giver.

May we today allow Jesus to breathe life again in us.

Meditate

From the origin of our time God spoke everything
into existence out of darkness.
Genesis 1

From the origin of our time God exhaled Jesus
speaking everything into existence out of darkness.

The Long Exhale began all life… and he today still
ignites life in mankind.

This present darkness cannot overcome that light.
John 1

Pray and Go

Eighty-five

Be still before God.
Exhale fully and let God fill you.

Meditate

Jesus, the Brilliant Light, walked on this earth, and
because of the darkness we had no idea.

Those of us who embrace him,
those of us who believe in who he is,
change families and are now the adopted daughters
and sons of God.

We can now come to the family table.

Daughters and Sons

Consider - John 1: 10 - 13

We have all heard the stories of a child who was abandoned, unwanted or homeless. Oh, the pain these children must feel in their loneliness. You may be one of them.

If so, my hope is that your story is now a good one; my hope is that you are now an adopted child of God.

We have also heard stories of generous families seeing the need of a lonely child and embracing them as if they were one of their own children. Often the story even moves to adoption.

Because of our sin this world is a dark place. We have all broken our relationship with the Father, and we, too, are homeless. We live on the side of darkness and cannot find our way back home.

Those of us who embrace and believe in Jesus actually change our families in this world from darkness to the side of Light. God makes us his own kids through Jesus. How beautiful!

Embrace Jesus.

Believe in who John says he is.

Enjoy being one of God's daughters. Enjoy being one of God's sons. Then walk right up to the family table. There is a place for you.

Meditate

Jesus, the Brilliant Light, walked on this earth, and
because of the darkness we had no idea.

Those of us who embrace him,
those of us who believe in who he is,
change families and are now the adopted daughters
and sons of God.

We can now come to the family table.

Pray and Go

Eighty-six

Be still before God.
Exhale fully and let God fill you.

Meditate

The Long Exhale of God jumped into our skin.
He experienced our experiences. He breathed the
same air.

He walked in our neighborhoods
and had dinner with us.

This is what God's glory looks like.
Jesus, our Brother, overflowed with grace;
he was 100% truth.

John the Baptizer, I, John the Writer and many
others testify to his story. Believe in Jesus with us.

God's Glory Looks Like

Consider - John 1: 14 - 18

Consider the possibility of God walking on the earth, not on some obscure section of a mountain or alone on a remote island, which he might do when no one is watching, but in our neighborhoods in plain sight.

Jesus walked with our ancestral neighbors in plain sight.

For the first thirty years of his life we are not told he did any miracles, although his birth was a miracle. We don't know that he healed anyone, or cast out any evil spirits, but we are told he looked like God's glory. It was not in his physical appearance, but in the words he spoke and in the way he lived.

Image living with God's glory. Seeing it daily in front of you.

Imagine growing up as a younger sibling to the One who was God's glory. Imagine living next door to the One who always overflowed with grace. Imagine working beside and having a lunch discussion with the One who not only spoke truth, but was truth. It was not until after his public baptism that he revealed this power through his teachings, his healing and his miracles. Yet he was always God's glory.

Jesus, the Long Exhale of God, walked with us.

This Brother of ours showed us what God's glory looks like.

John the Writer witnessed his glory. Believe.

Meditate

The Long Exhale of God jumped into our skin.
He experienced our experiences. He breathed the
same air.

He walked in our neighborhoods
and had dinner with us.

This is what God's glory looks like.
Jesus, our Brother, overflowed with grace;
he was 100% truth.

I, John, testify to his story. Believe.

Pray and Go

Thank you!

Thank you for taking this journey toward "Finding John's Jesus." Jesus transformed John's life, and he is transforming us too. We are lives being changed by Jesus.

May you know you are deeply loved by our God and that he has work for you, not someday, but today.

May we turn from our sinful ways, believe in Jesus for our rescue and follow him.

Life is in Jesus. Believe.

Peace.

Bio

The author, in his life work, is trying to faithfully live out his personal creed "to know God and help others know him too."

Scott currently works as a Sports Chaplain and Character Coach with student-athletes at Franklin and Marshall College in the city of Lancaster, Pennsylvania, with the CCO (Coalition for Christian Outreach www.ccojubilee.org).

Endnotes

The passages of Scripture have been condensed and paraphrased to help readers meditate on the accounts of Jesus John the Writer had the privilege to witness.

A special thanks to Apple, Inc. for the graphics in "Pages."